AF419825

# VEXTURE

# Vexture

DERRICK C SOLANO

# Contents

For the ones who were told they were too broken to be fixed, too damaged to be loved, or too lost to be found. This book is for you—the ones who wear their scars like armor, who fight battles no one else can see, and who keep standing even when the world tries to knock them down. To those who refuse to break, this is your anthem.

# Chapter 1: Why Here?

Let's get something straight right out of the gate: if you're here, you're likely pissed off, lost, or questioning why the hell life dealt you the hand it did. You've probably been told to "move on" or "just let it go" more times than you can count. And it's infuriating, right? Because people don't get it. Not really. They don't get how life can sometimes feel like a game you weren't even invited to play, where everyone else seems to have the rulebook, and you're just left winging it, somehow always on the losing side.

Here's the truth that no one else wants to say out loud: **you have every right to be angry**. Angry at the world, at your past, at the people who let you down. Hell, even angry at yourself for the times you messed up. This isn't about shaming you for what you feel or pretending it's not there. It's about giving those feelings the respect they deserve, not because they're pleasant, but because they're *real*. This anger and pain didn't come out of nowhere; it's a direct result of what you've been through. And until you face it, it'll just keep festering, like an infection no one's willing to treat.

Maybe you're feeling lost because life pulled you in every direction but the one that's truly yours. And there's this weight, this undeniable heaviness that comes with feeling like you're just floating through life, unmoored, with no solid ground to stand on. Like you're in some waiting room, unsure of when—or even if—you'll be called into the life you were meant to live.

And the irony? People want you to hurry up and "find yourself," as if it's some magical scavenger hunt where you just pick up pieces of yourself along the way. But what they don't tell you is that sometimes, in order to find yourself, you have to confront everything that's broken, lost, or shattered inside. That's the part most people skip over because it's damn uncomfortable. But I won't. I won't skip it because I know exactly how crucial it is to dig deep, to get uncomfortable, to acknowledge every ugly feeling you've tried to push down.

This book isn't here to smooth over your anger or make it prettier. It's here to take that anger and make it fuel, to turn it into something useful. You're not broken for feeling this way, and it's about time someone told you that. You're here because you've been through something, because you've been to hell and back, and every scar, every painful memory is a testament to that. So, let's start with that foundation—the acknowledgment that you're here because life isn't all sunshine and roses, and that's okay.

Let me introduce you to a new concept—one that's probably going to feel a little uncomfortable, maybe even a little foreign at first. I call it **vexture**. It's not some made-up word just for the sake of being clever; it's a mindset, a way of being, and if you let it, it'll become your lifeline. See, vexture is about taking all those dark, heavy things inside—the pain, the scars, the anger—and layering them into something solid, something that doesn't just hold up but becomes damn near indestructible. It's the art of layering your pain until it doesn't just sit there, rotting in the corner of your mind, but instead forms a foundation so strong nothing can shake you.

Why "vexture"? Because there's this thing about strength that most people get wrong. They think being strong means staying untouched, unscarred, looking like they've had it easy. But real strength is textured—it's got edges and layers, and yes, it's been hurt, it's been broken, it's been scarred. Vexture is strength that's been through the fire, that's seen darkness, and come out the other side. It's the resilience you gain by being brave enough to face the things that make most people run.

This isn't about pretending the past didn't happen or that the pain wasn't real. It's about acknowledging every single experience—every wound, every scar—as part of who you are. Think about it like building armor. Each painful memory, each heartbreak, each time you got knocked down and found a way to stand up, that's a piece of your armor. Over time, with each layer of hurt that you embrace instead of avoiding, you're adding to that armor, making it thicker, stronger, and damn near impenetrable.

But here's the thing: vexture isn't about hiding behind that armor, pretending nothing can hurt you anymore. It's about standing with your scars visible, not giving a damn who sees them, and daring life to throw something harder because you've already built a foundation that can take it. It's about looking at every piece of trauma, every inch of anger or fear, and saying, "This isn't going to break me. This is going to make me unbreakable."

Vexture is the process of letting yourself be layered by life's hardest hits and letting each layer make you stronger. It's what happens when you stop trying to forget your past and start using it. Think of it like scar tissue—when skin gets hurt, it grows back thicker, tougher. And the more scars, the stronger the protection. That's what vexture is: a patchwork of survival, a collage of resilience. And the beauty of it is that it's uniquely yours. No two people's vexture looks the same, because no two people have the same scars. This process of layering strength through every hurt, every betrayal, every struggle is yours alone. It's personal, it's raw, and it's real.

You might be wondering why you'd even want to carry around the weight of your scars. Here's why: because those scars are yours. They're proof of every single thing you survived. People who try to "forget" their pain or push it down, they're just ticking time bombs. That pain doesn't disappear; it festers, it finds ways to leak into everything else. But when you accept it, when you give those scars a purpose, they stop being wounds and start being armor. They become something you own instead of something that owns you.

Vexture isn't easy. It's not a quick fix or a "let's pretend it's all better" solution. It's a brutal process of sitting with your pain, of accepting every part of yourself, and learning to see strength in things that used to make you feel weak. This isn't going to be the kind of book where I tell you to "just let go" of your pain, because for some of us, letting go isn't an option. And maybe it doesn't need to be. Maybe, instead of letting go, you just need to let it settle, layer by layer, until it forms something solid.

Because here's the truth: if you let it, your pain can be the thing that frees you. Vexture is about knowing that your scars aren't setbacks; they're stepping stones. And if you're willing to look at them as such, if you're willing to let them become part of you, then they will no longer have the power to hold you back. Instead, they'll become the source of your strength, proof that you don't just survive—you evolve. You adapt. You become something stronger than anything life throws your way.

So, if you're ready, let's start layering. Let's start building that vexture.

Here's a hard truth, and it might be uncomfortable to hear: you're not here to be "fixed." You're not some broken-down piece of machinery that just needs a quick tune-up to get back to perfect working order. Because let's face it, there is no going back to perfect—*perfect never existed*. And every time we try to reach some idealized version of ourselves that's untouched by pain or hardship, we end up further away from who we truly are. Trying to "fix" ourselves is a losing game because it implies that there's something wrong with us, something fundamentally flawed or incomplete. And I'm here to tell you that's just not true.

What we're doing here, what this whole concept of vexture is about, isn't "fixing" anything. It's about **layering**. Layering strength through scars, not because they're problems to be erased, but because they're proof of life lived, battles fought, and survival earned. Those scars aren't imperfections—they're badges. Each one represents something you've overcome, something that tried to take you down and didn't succeed. Every scar is a story, and each story is a layer of strength you carry with you. They don't make you weaker; they make you

*you.* And the minute you stop trying to erase them is the minute you start using them.

Think about it: trying to "fix" ourselves is exhausting. It's chasing an illusion that was never real to begin with. Life isn't about finding a version of ourselves that doesn't feel pain or sadness or anger. Those emotions, those experiences—they're part of the human condition. They're part of what makes us who we are. So rather than going on some pointless crusade to "get rid" of the pain, what if we just embraced it? What if we let it make us stronger?

Layering strength isn't about reaching some end goal where everything is magically better. It's about accepting that life will keep throwing punches, and every time it does, you're going to get back up—sometimes battered, sometimes bruised, but always stronger than before. Because each hit leaves a mark, and each mark becomes another layer of resilience. It's not about being immune to pain; it's about knowing that no matter how many times life knocks you down, you're not going to stay there. You've built yourself out of those hits, out of those scars, and each one has added to your unbreakable core.

When you stop trying to "fix" yourself, you free yourself. You free yourself from the endless pressure to be something you're not, to fit into a mold that was never made for you. And you start to build from a place of honesty, a place that recognizes all the shit you've been through and gives it a purpose. You stop hiding from the parts of yourself that feel too messy or too damaged, and you let them be part of the foundation you're creating. And here's the beauty of it: when you layer strength instead of chasing some mythical "fixed" version of yourself, you build a foundation that no one else can touch. It's yours, created from your scars, and it doesn't need anyone else's approval to exist.

So, let's put it all on the table. This isn't a book about healing in the way most people think of it. It's not about getting rid of the pain. It's about learning how to live with it, how to let it make you stronger, and how to recognize that every scar you carry is a part of your journey. When you layer your strength, you stop seeing your past as a collection of mistakes or things that went wrong. You start to see it as the blueprint for your resilience.

This isn't easy work. There are going to be moments when it feels like too much, when the weight of it all seems like more than you can handle. But that's exactly when you know you're doing it right—because building strength isn't comfortable. It's messy, it's hard, and it forces you to face parts of yourself that you'd rather leave buried. But in doing that, in facing every part of who you are, you find something real. You find a version of yourself that isn't just trying to get by but is actively creating a life built on strength and resilience.

And that's what vexture is. It's letting go of the lie that you need to be "fixed" and embracing the truth that you're already whole—scars and all. It's turning every experience, every bit of pain, into a layer that protects you, that defines you, and that no one else can take away. It's not about fixing anything; it's about building something that can't be broken.

If there's one message to drive home here, it's this: you're not here to "fix" yourself; you're here to rebuild, to create something so solid that no one and nothing can tear it down. Because here's the thing about rebuilding: it acknowledges that life has taken its toll, that the foundation you started with might have been shaky or even destroyed, but that doesn't mean you're done. It doesn't mean you're broken beyond repair. Rebuilding isn't about erasing the past or pretending things didn't go wrong; it's about picking up every broken piece and creating something new, something stronger.

When you decide to rebuild, you're not starting over from scratch; you're starting over from experience. And that experience? That's priceless. It's knowing what it feels like to hit rock bottom and realizing that even at your lowest, you survived. You found a way to keep going, to keep breathing, even when every part of you wanted to give up. And that's not weakness—that's strength, pure and simple. That's something no one can take from you, no matter what happens.

Rebuilding means accepting that you don't have to go back to the person you were before life knocked you down. You don't have to "recover" to some imaginary state of perfection where you're untouched by pain. That's not real, and chasing it is a waste of your time and energy. Instead, rebuilding is about taking every scar, every painful memory, every single hardship and saying, "This is mine. I own this. And I'm going to use it to make something unbreakable."

Think about it like a house. Maybe you started with a foundation that was cracked, or walls that were unstable, or a roof that couldn't withstand the storms life threw at it. Eventually, it all came crashing down, and here you are, standing among the ruins. Most people would look at the rubble and say, "It's over. There's no fixing this." But you? You're different. You're looking at the ruins and thinking, "Alright, let's rebuild."

When you rebuild, you don't ignore the wreckage—you use it. Every broken beam, every cracked brick, every piece of rubble becomes part of the new foundation. And this time, you build it your way. You don't follow anyone else's blueprint or let anyone else tell you what it should look like. You take your experiences, your pain, your scars, and you make them part of the structure. Because now you know where the weak points were, and you're not about to make the same mistakes again.

The beauty of rebuilding is that you're creating something that's entirely yours. It's not a patched-up version of what once was; it's a new creation, fortified by everything you've been through. This isn't about trying to put the pieces back together exactly as they were. It's about using those pieces to create something stronger, something that can withstand the storms because it's built from them. And in doing that, you're not just building a life—you're building *your* life, a life that's been reforged in fire and strengthened through every trial.

When you rebuild, you're acknowledging that the past matters, but it doesn't define your future. You're taking control, deciding that no matter what has happened, you get to decide what comes next. And that's power. That's real, unfiltered, unapologetic power. It's saying, "I am not my past. I am what I build from it."

And that's why we're not here to "fix" anything. We're here to rebuild. Because fixing implies that something was broken beyond use, something to be discarded. But when you rebuild, you're not discarding anything. You're using every experience, every bit of pain, and turning it into strength. You're layering it, letting each piece add to the foundation until it's something no one can touch. This is a journey of resilience, of strength, and of ownership. And at the end of it, you're not just going to be standing on your own two feet—you're going to be unstoppable.

You're here to rebuild because you're tired of pretending the past didn't happen, tired of patching up cracks that go deeper than anyone else can see. You're here because you know that the only way forward is to take every painful memory, every scar, and let it become part of something unbreakable. This isn't about fixing. This is about creating. It's about taking what life has thrown at you and using it to build something that's yours, something that no one else can take from you.

This is where we start. Not with a plan to fix the past, but with a commitment to rebuild the future, one scar, one layer at a time.

# Chapter 2: Sit in It

If there's one truth about pain that nobody talks about, it's that feeling it—really letting yourself feel it—is one of the hardest things you'll ever do. Most people don't want to feel their pain, don't want to acknowledge the depths of their own hurt, and it's understandable. Pain isn't pretty. It's raw, it's uncomfortable, and it has a way of exposing things we'd rather keep hidden. But if you want to build resilience, if you want to truly understand yourself and find a way forward, you have to do what most people avoid: *you have to sit in it.*

Sitting with your pain isn't the same as wallowing in it. Let's make that distinction clear. Wallowing is when you drown in your own misery without looking for a way out; it's letting your pain define you, letting it consume everything you are. But sitting with it? That's different. Sitting with your pain means being brave enough to face it without judgment, without distraction, without pretending it's not there. It means stopping long enough to actually feel everything you've been trying to ignore, to let yourself cry, scream, shake—whatever you need to do to fully experience it.

We live in a world obsessed with numbing. People numb out with social media, alcohol, drugs, food, TV—you name it. Anything to keep from facing the uncomfortable, the scary, the painful parts of life. But the problem with numbing is that it doesn't erase the pain; it just buries it. It stuffs it down, but buried pain doesn't disappear. It festers, it grows, and it finds ways to sneak back into your life, often when you least expect it. So, if you're done running, if you're ready to face the things that hurt the most, then the first step is learning to sit with that pain.

Here's the brutal truth: sitting with your pain is going to feel like shit. It's going to hurt. It's going to feel uncomfortable, maybe even unbearable at times. But pain, when you give it the space to be felt, eventually transforms. It doesn't stay raw and jagged forever. Like a storm, it has its peak, and then it fades. But you won't get to that part if you keep running. You won't ever find peace if you keep covering up the hurt with quick fixes and distractions. Pain has a way of demanding to be felt, and the longer you avoid it, the louder it becomes.

So, how do you sit with it? You start by giving yourself permission to feel everything without trying to make sense of it or push it away. Sit in a quiet space, away from distractions. Let the feelings come up without filtering them. Maybe it's grief, maybe it's anger, maybe it's a hopelessness that's been lurking just below the surface. Whatever it is, let it rise. Notice how your body responds—do you tense up? Do you feel a weight in your chest, a tightness in your throat? These physical sensations are part of the process; they're your body's way of releasing the pain you've been holding onto.

It might help to say it out loud: "This is painful. This hurts. I feel this." Acknowledge it. Because that's what so many of us are afraid to do—to admit that we're hurting, to admit that we're not okay. But acknowledging it doesn't make you weak; it makes you real. It makes you human. Sitting with pain doesn't mean you're giving up or letting it take over your life. It means you're honoring the experiences that have shaped you, giving them a voice instead of silencing them.

People often avoid pain because they think if they start crying, if they start really feeling it, they'll never stop. But emotions don't work like that. They're temporary, like waves. They rise, they break, and then they recede. When you sit with your pain, you're letting that wave crash over you, trusting that it'll subside, trusting that you'll still be standing when it does. And when you allow yourself to fully experience that wave, it loses its power over you. It becomes something you've acknowledged, something you've survived, rather than something lurking in the background, waiting to take you down.

Think of this as emotional training. Just like a muscle builds strength through resistance, your emotional resilience builds through facing discomfort. Every time you sit with your pain, every time you allow yourself to feel it without judgment or escape, you're strengthening your ability to handle whatever life throws your way. You're teaching yourself that no matter how much it hurts, you can survive it. You can feel it, you can let it break over you, and you can still keep going.

This isn't an overnight fix. It's a practice, a commitment to yourself. Sitting with pain is something you'll return to again and again, each time finding a little more strength, a little more resilience. It's an act of bravery, of defiance, to sit with the things that hurt rather than turning away. Because by facing them, you're stripping them of their power. You're showing yourself that you don't need to run, that you don't need to hide. You're stronger than that.

So here's your first task: the next time you feel that pang of sadness, that wave of anger, that ache of loneliness, don't reach for the distractions. Don't numb it with mindless scrolling or a drink or anything else. Just sit. Feel it. Let it rise and know that it's not here to consume you—it's here to be felt, to be honored, and to eventually be released. This is the first step in taking back your life, one raw, unfiltered feeling at a time.

Here's the irony of pain: the more you avoid it, the more it takes over. Avoidance feels like a solution, but it's really just a trap, a way of locking yourself into a cycle where the pain is constantly waiting, lurking just beneath the surface, never really gone. The thing is, pain is relentless. It's like water seeping into the cracks of a dam—ignore it long enough, and eventually, it'll break through with a force that's impossible to contain. And when that happens, you're left dealing with a flood you can't control, a surge of emotions you're not prepared to face all at once.

When you avoid pain, you're giving it free rein to take over every part of your life. It starts to show up in places you wouldn't expect—in your relationships, in your work, in your health. It's the reason people snap at loved ones for no apparent reason, why they struggle to focus or feel exhausted even after a full night's sleep. It's the reason some people feel a constant sense of unease, like there's a weight pressing on their chest that they can't explain. All of that? That's buried pain, pain that's been shoved down so many times it's found other ways to make itself known.

Avoiding pain doesn't make it disappear; it just makes it louder. But here's where it gets interesting: pain, when acknowledged, loses some of its bite. When you stop running and turn to face it, you start to see it for what it really is—a part of you, yes, but not all of you. It's an experience, a memory, an emotion. It's real, and it's valid, but it doesn't have to control you. And once you see it this way, once you realize that pain is just as temporary as any other feeling, you can start to channel it instead of letting it consume you.

So, how do you channel it? First, you have to recognize that pain is energy. Raw, intense energy. Think about it—when you're in pain, your body is flooded with emotion, with adrenaline, with a need for release. That's why people scream, cry, or punch walls when they're overwhelmed; it's their body's way of discharging that energy. But instead of letting it explode in ways that only bring more chaos, you can take that energy and use it to fuel something constructive. Pain, when harnessed, is one of the most powerful motivators you'll ever experience.

Let's say you're dealing with betrayal. Someone you trusted completely let you down, maybe even shattered your sense of self. That pain feels all-consuming, like it's taking up every inch of your mind, leaving you bitter and angry. But rather than letting that betrayal twist you into someone you don't recognize, someone constantly guarded and resentful, you can use that pain to fuel self-respect and boundaries. You can let that experience remind you of your worth, to reinforce the fact that you deserve loyalty and honesty. Instead of allowing betrayal to tear you down, you can let it become the foundation for stronger relationships—relationships built on respect, because now you know exactly what you won't tolerate.

Channeling pain is about transforming it into fuel for whatever you need in that moment. If you're feeling abandoned, let that pain push you to build a stronger sense of self, to find comfort within instead of constantly searching for it outside. If you're angry, use that anger to drive you toward change, to create a life that's truly yours. Pain, when used this way, stops being a weight that drags you down and becomes a force that propels you forward. It's not about ignoring what happened or pretending it didn't hurt—it's about using that hurt as motivation to build a life you don't need to escape from.

Pain can be a teacher if you let it. It can show you what matters, what you value, and what you're willing to fight for. When you channel your pain, you're essentially reclaiming control over your own life. You're saying, "Yes, this hurt. But I'm going to decide what to do with it." That's power. That's taking something that could destroy you and turning it into the reason you keep going. It's not easy, and it's not instant, but every time you choose to channel your pain instead of avoiding it, you're reinforcing the idea that you are stronger than the things that try to break you.

This doesn't mean the pain disappears overnight. It'll still be there, it'll still hurt, but you'll be in control of it, rather than letting it control you. When you feel that wave of pain rising, instead of pushing it down or running from it, ask yourself, "What can I use this for? How can this make me stronger?" Maybe it drives you to create, to write, to exercise, to make art, or to reach out to someone who's struggling. Pain is a powerful connector; it's something we all understand on some level. When you channel it, you're not just helping yourself—you're turning your pain into something that can resonate, that can impact others.

Here's the takeaway: pain, left unchecked, is destructive. It'll erode you from the inside out, leaving you bitter, angry, and lost. But pain, when channeled, is transformative. It's the kind of fuel that can take you to places you never thought possible. So the next time you feel that familiar ache, that sting of disappointment or betrayal, don't reach for distractions. Don't numb it. Instead, sit with it, let it be, and then ask yourself how you can use it. Because pain is inevitable, but whether it controls you or fuels you? That's your choice.

Let's clear something up right now: sitting with your pain doesn't mean drowning in it. There's a fine line between allowing yourself to feel and letting yourself spiral, and knowing that difference can be the difference between healing and getting stuck. Because let's be honest—when you're hurting, when the weight of everything feels like it's pressing down on you, it's easy to sink into it. It's easy to let yourself fall into a pattern of self-pity, of believing that the pain will never end, that this is just how it is now. But that's not sitting with your pain—that's wallowing, and wallowing is just as destructive as avoiding.

Wallowing is when you start to let the pain define you, when you let it become the center of your world. It's when you're not just feeling hurt—you're reliving it, replaying every terrible thing that happened, making it the soundtrack to your life. Wallowing is self-pity on repeat. It's telling yourself that you're stuck, that things will never get better, that you're helpless against what's happened to you. And while there's a place for letting yourself feel the depth of your pain, wallowing takes it too far. Wallowing keeps you in a loop where the hurt becomes part of your identity, where it starts to color everything else in your life.

Understanding, on the other hand, is different. Understanding is acknowledging the pain, recognizing its impact, and giving yourself the time and space to process it—but without letting it consume you. It's about stepping back and saying, "Yes, this happened. Yes, it hurt. But it doesn't have to own me." When you understand your pain, you're looking at it from a distance, seeing it as part of your story, not the whole story. Understanding is about finding a way to use that pain as fuel, as a source of power that propels you forward instead of holding you back.

Think of it like this: when you wallow, you're letting pain be the driver. It's the one steering, dictating where you go, how you feel, what you do. But when you understand your pain, you're the one behind the wheel. You're in control, choosing how to navigate it, deciding when to lean into it and when to let it rest. Pain isn't leading the way—you are. And when you're the one in control, you can choose to use that pain to push you in the direction you want to go. You can choose to take that anger, that sadness, that disappointment, and turn it into something meaningful.

So, how do you make that shift from wallowing to understanding? It starts with a mindset change. You stop asking, "Why did this happen to me?" and start asking, "What can I learn from this?" It's a small shift, but it changes everything. When you're stuck in the "why," you're focused on the past, on what's already happened and can't be undone. But when you ask, "What can I learn?" you're looking to the future, to what you can take from this experience to make you stronger. It's no longer about feeling helpless—it's about finding purpose in the pain, about letting it become something that serves you rather than something that controls you.

Let's say you've been through a breakup that tore you apart. Maybe you're tempted to wallow, to replay every painful moment, every hurtful word, until it becomes all you can think about. But what if, instead, you looked at that breakup and thought, "Okay, this happened. It hurt like hell. But what can I learn here?" Maybe you learn that you deserve someone who respects you, that you need to set better boundaries, that you're capable of moving forward even when it feels impossible. When you choose to understand rather than wallow, you're taking that experience and making it a stepping stone instead of a dead end.

Using pain as fuel is about letting every hard experience, every scar, every hurt become part of your drive. It's about making the conscious choice to let it push you forward rather than pull you back. Pain, when understood, can become one of your most powerful motivators. It's a reminder of what you've survived, a testament to your resilience, and a source of energy that can propel you toward something better. Instead of letting it weigh you down, you let it lift you up. You turn it into a fire that burns so bright, it lights the way even on your darkest days.

This doesn't mean you ignore the pain or pretend it's not there. Quite the opposite—it means you acknowledge it fully, you feel every bit of it, but you don't stop there. You take that pain and ask, "How can I use this?" Maybe it pushes you to be more compassionate, to help others who are struggling. Maybe it drives you to create something—art, music, writing—that expresses what you're going through. Maybe it becomes the reason you start working harder, setting goals, building a life that feels meaningful. Pain, when used as fuel, becomes a catalyst for change rather than a sentence to suffering.

Here's the bottom line: pain is inevitable, but how you handle it is up to you. You can let it keep you stuck, or you can use it to build something stronger. You can let it define you, or you can use it to redefine yourself. When you choose to understand rather than wallow, you're taking control of your own story. You're saying, "This hurt, but it's not going to break me. It's going to build me."

So, the next time you feel that wave of pain, that familiar ache, don't let it spiral into wallowing. Take a step back. Look at it. Acknowledge it. And then ask yourself, "How can I use this? What can this pain teach me? How can it make me stronger?" Because once you start using pain as fuel, you're no longer at its mercy—you're in control, and that's where true resilience begins.

Let's talk about letting emotions rise up without slapping them down, minimizing them, or beating yourself up for feeling them. This is the part where we don't hold back, where we let those buried emotions come to the surface, raw and unfiltered, and sit with them—really *sit* with them. This isn't the time for self-censorship or trying to be the "strong" version of yourself that doesn't need to cry, rage, or feel. This is the time for facing whatever emotions are there and letting them just be.

Here's the thing: society has this twisted way of shaming us for feeling anything other than happy. We're told to "look on the bright side," to "let it go," to "be positive"—and all that does is tell us that our feelings are somehow wrong or that we're weak for having them. So, let's strip that crap away. Feeling your emotions doesn't make you weak; it makes you *alive*. Every emotion—anger, sadness, fear, even despair—is a part of you that's demanding attention. Ignoring it doesn't make it go away. It just stores it, lets it fester, and trust me, it's going to find its way out eventually, whether you like it or not.

So here's your new goal: let those emotions surface without judging them. Allow yourself to feel them fully without labeling them as "bad" or "weak" or "wrong." And to do this, we're going to get real and set up some "sit-down-and-fucking-feel-it" practices. This isn't about wallowing, remember—it's about understanding and processing.

## Technique #1: The Rage Room (or the DIY Version)

If you've got some serious anger simmering under the surface, sometimes the best thing you can do is let it out physically. You don't have to break the bank or find a literal "rage room" to do this—there's plenty of ways to make your own version. Find a safe, private space where you can release that energy. Grab a pillow and scream into it, punch it, throw it. Get some old plates from a thrift store, go outside (safely), and smash them. Use your body to release all that pent-up energy. Anger is physical—*let it out physically*.

This isn't about "getting over it" in one session. It's about giving your anger space to breathe, about letting yourself be unapologetically pissed off. When you give yourself permission to release that anger, it becomes less overwhelming. You stop carrying it around like a weight strapped to your chest, and instead, you let it move through you. And if anyone tells you that screaming, smashing, or pounding your pillow is "overreacting," remind yourself that you're the one doing the real work, facing your pain instead of ignoring it.

## Technique #2: The Raw Truth Journal

If sadness or grief is what's coming up, try journaling—*but not the fluffy, gratitude kind.* This isn't about looking on the bright side or trying to spin things in a positive light. This is about raw honesty. Get a notebook you don't mind filling with anger, sadness, bitterness—whatever it is that needs a voice. Set a timer, maybe for 15 or 20 minutes, and just write. Don't filter yourself. Don't worry about grammar, about making sense, or about who might read it someday. This is just for you, a place to spill everything without holding back.

Let the words flow. If you need to write "I'm so angry" or "I hate this" over and over, do it. If you're sad, if you feel empty, if you feel lost—write that too. This journal is your space to be as real as possible, to confront the parts of yourself that you don't show to the world. When you get it down on paper, you're taking some of that heaviness out of your mind and letting it exist in a place where you can see it. It's a release, and sometimes just the act of seeing your pain written out is enough to lighten the load a bit.

## Technique #3: The "Sit with It" Meditation

Now, this one is hard. If you're ready to go deep, this is the technique that'll get you there. Find a quiet space where you won't be interrupted. Sit down, close your eyes, and breathe. Let whatever emotions you've been avoiding start to come up.

Don't force anything—just be still and breathe, allowing whatever feelings arise to do so. Maybe you'll feel anger, maybe sadness, maybe a mix of everything. The key here is to let the emotions come without trying to change them or push them away.

Here's what will probably happen: your mind is going to fight this. It's going to want to distract you, to get up, to do anything but feel the uncomfortable sensations in your body. But don't give in. Sit with it. Feel the heaviness, the tension, the heat, whatever sensations come up. Let your body experience it. And remember, this isn't permanent. Emotions are like waves—they rise, they peak, and then they recede. Trust that even the most intense feelings will eventually pass if you let them.

## Technique #4: The Soundtrack Surrender

Sometimes, music can unlock feelings that words can't. Create a playlist that matches your mood, that resonates with whatever you're feeling. If you're angry, choose songs that feel raw, that help you connect with that fire. If you're sad, find songs that reflect that sadness. Sit down, put on your headphones, and let the music guide you. Don't just listen—*feel* it. Cry if you need to. Scream if you need to. Let the music carry you to the places you've been too afraid to go on your own.

This isn't about cheering yourself up or finding a happy ending. This is about release, about letting the music help you express things you might not have words for. Music has a way of accessing the parts of us that we keep hidden, the parts that are hard to explain. Let it be a tool for letting out what you can't say, for connecting with the emotions that are hardest to face.

---

Each of these practices is about one thing: facing your emotions without shame, without judgment, and without fear. You're not here to label them as "bad" or "wrong." You're here to let them be, to give them space, and in doing that, to take away some of their power. This is how you start to own your pain instead of letting it own you. When you can sit with those feelings, let them surface, and let them be—without needing to fix or hide or numb—you're reclaiming control over your life.

It's not easy, and there will be times when you want to turn away, to escape. But every time you sit with it, every time you let yourself feel, you're building strength, layer by layer. You're learning that you can handle whatever life throws at you. This is how you become resilient—by facing the things that others run from, by giving yourself the space to feel without shame, without judgment, and without fear.

# Chapter 3: Break the Loop

If you're here, it's probably because you're done living in survival mode. And yet, breaking free from it isn't as simple as deciding you're done. When you've been through hell—when trauma, betrayal, and hardship have become your normal—your mind adapts to keep you alive. It builds habits, creates loops, and sets you in patterns that feel safe, even if they're actually keeping you trapped. This is survival mode, and while it might have kept you afloat when you needed it, it's not where you're meant to stay.

Survival mode is like being stuck in a loop. It's a way of living that keeps you constantly on guard, constantly ready for the worst to happen, because, for a long time, the worst was a regular part of your life. Maybe you learned to always expect betrayal, so now you can't fully trust anyone. Or maybe you learned to shut down your emotions to avoid getting hurt, so now you're numb even when you want to feel connected. Trauma has a way of building walls around you, walls that were necessary once but are now keeping you from moving forward.

The first step to breaking out of this loop is recognizing it—seeing these patterns for what they are. And the tough part? It's being honest with yourself about the habits you've developed to survive. These patterns can look like anything from constantly doubting people's intentions to isolating yourself because being close to others feels like a risk. It's shutting down at the first sign of conflict or pushing people away before they can get too close. And here's where it gets tricky: survival patterns can feel like "protecting yourself," but what they're really doing is keeping you isolated, alone, and stuck.

Let's call it what it is: these loops are traps. They keep you in a cycle where the only goal is getting through the day without getting hurt again. It's a way of existing, but it's not a way of living. When you're in survival mode, everything is reactive. You're not choosing your life; you're just reacting to it, always braced for impact. This constant state of hyper-awareness might make you feel safe, but it's a false safety. Because while you're busy guarding yourself, you're also keeping out anything good—love, joy, peace, connection. Survival mode is all about minimizing risk, but in doing that, it also minimizes everything that makes life worth living.

Recognizing these trauma patterns requires brutal honesty. It means looking at the habits and beliefs you've held onto as shields and asking yourself if they're still serving you. Do you assume the worst about people because you were betrayed before? Do you avoid intimacy because someone once used your vulnerability against you? Do you keep yourself busy, constantly distracted, because slowing down might mean facing the pain? These are hard questions, but until you face them, you'll stay in the loop. You'll stay stuck, always surviving but never really living.

Here's an example: maybe you grew up in a home where love came with strings attached, where you learned that to be cared for, you had to be useful, perfect, or compliant. So now, as an adult, you find yourself over-giving, always trying to prove your worth, always afraid that if you're not doing enough, people will abandon you. This is a trauma pattern. It's a loop that's kept you in survival mode, where love is conditional and where being yourself feels like a risk. And until you see this pattern for what it is, it'll keep running your life.

Recognizing trauma patterns is a form of self-awareness, and it's the first step to breaking free. Once you start noticing these loops, you can begin to understand that they're not you. They're coping mechanisms you developed to survive, and at one point, they served you well. But now, they're holding you back. Breaking out of survival mode is about realizing that you don't have to live as if the world is out to get you, as if love is a threat, as if happiness is something you're not allowed to have.

This is where the real work begins. Once you see the pattern, you can choose to disrupt it. You can catch yourself in those moments when you're about to retreat, when you're about to push someone away, and you can choose to do something different. You can start creating new patterns, patterns that are based on living, not just surviving. But first, you have to see the loop for what it is—a cage built to keep you safe but that now keeps you stuck.

Let's get real: breaking these patterns isn't just hard; it's terrifying. I know because I've lived it, fought it, and still, sometimes, I find myself right back at the start, wrestling with the same damn loops. These trauma patterns aren't things you snap out of overnight. They're deep, they're ingrained, and they're sneaky. They're the quiet whispers that tell you it's safer to pull back, to shut down, to avoid. And to break that cycle? You have to be willing to confront the parts of yourself that feel safest hiding.

One of my earliest memories of survival mode was right after being adopted. I'd been bounced from place to place, and each move left its mark. By the time I was placed with my adoptive family, I was already learning not to get too comfortable, not to trust that this new place would stick. And sure enough, the conditions of that home were anything but safe. I started to build a shell, shutting down my feelings because showing any sign of vulnerability felt like inviting trouble. I learned quickly that trust was a luxury I couldn't afford. And so, that survival loop began—guard everything, expect nothing, stay on edge.

It's hard to explain to someone who hasn't lived it what it feels like to carry that weight day after day. The constant pressure, the endless suspicion, the way even happiness feels dangerous, like a setup for the next fall. But there was one moment that stands out, a time when I had to make a choice: stay stuck in survival mode, or take a risk and break free. It was after I lost my son. That pain was different; it was soul-shattering, the kind that leaves you feeling like you'll never be whole again. And in the aftermath, I wanted nothing more than to go numb, to retreat back into that familiar shell where nothing and no one could reach me. Because if I didn't care, I couldn't be hurt, right?

But something in me snapped. Maybe it was the realization that survival mode hadn't actually saved me from anything—it had only kept me from feeling. And when you're in that much pain, the numbness doesn't help; it only makes you feel like you're disappearing, like the pain has swallowed you whole. So, I made a choice. I chose to face it, to break the loop. It wasn't pretty, and it wasn't easy. It meant confronting a lot of anger, a lot of bitterness, and a whole lot of grief. But I knew that if I didn't, if I kept hiding behind that wall, I'd never get out of that cage. I'd never really live.

Breaking the loop meant learning to trust again, even when every part of me screamed that trust was a risk I couldn't take. It meant letting people in, one small step at a time, even when the instinct to push them away was overwhelming. And it meant forgiving—not the people who hurt me, but myself. Forgiving myself for all the times I'd shut down, for all the relationships I'd sabotaged, for all the moments I'd let fear drive me. Because that's what survival mode does; it keeps you so locked up in fear that you don't even realize how much of life you're missing.

I won't lie to you and say that I never slip back into those patterns. Sometimes, when things get hard, that instinct to shut down, to retreat, still creeps in. But now I recognize it. I see it for what it is—a remnant of my past, a habit born out of pain. And instead of letting it control me, I confront it. I choose to push past it. Because that's what breaking the loop is about: choosing, over and over again, to live differently. It's about deciding every day that you're not going to let fear, or anger, or pain dictate your life.

These moments of breaking the cycle are brutal. They're uncomfortable. They bring up all the things you'd rather leave buried. But in those moments, you're reclaiming yourself.

You're taking back control from the patterns that once controlled you. And each time you do it, each time you confront that instinct to shut down and choose to stay open instead, you're building a new loop—a loop that's about resilience, not just survival. You're creating a life that's not about avoiding pain but about embracing strength.

That's the heart of this journey. It's knowing that, yes, you've been through hell, and those survival patterns kept you safe when you needed them. But you don't need them anymore. They're not keeping you safe now; they're keeping you stuck. And the only way forward is to choose, over and over, to break the cycle. To face the darkness, to confront the hurt, and to let yourself live beyond survival.

Once you've recognized the patterns that survival mode has locked you into, and once you've decided to break free, the question becomes: *How?* How do you take something as heavy as trauma and make it a catalyst for change instead of a cage that keeps you trapped? The truth is, it's a process, and it's one that requires consistency, grit, and a willingness to face the parts of yourself that you might want to leave in the dark. But the payoff is worth it, because when you turn trauma into a catalyst, you're finally using it as fuel rather than letting it keep you chained.

Here are some straightforward, no-bullshit strategies for flipping the switch on trauma so it propels you forward instead of holding you back.

## Tip #1: Confront the Story

The story you tell yourself about your trauma can either trap you or set you free. If your story is one of helplessness, of being the victim who had no choice, then it becomes a loop, a narrative that keeps you stuck in the past. But if you confront that story, if you challenge it, you can start to see yourself as more than just a victim. This doesn't mean denying the pain or pretending it didn't happen; it means acknowledging that, yes, it was hard, yes, it was unfair—but that you are not defined by that moment. The goal here is to reframe your story so that you're not powerless in it. Instead, make yourself the one who survived, who chose to rise up, who found strength in the darkest places.

One way to do this is through journaling. Write down the story you've been telling yourself, the narrative that's been looping in your mind. And then, rewrite it. Write it from the perspective of someone who didn't just survive, but who emerged stronger. Write it as the person who took that pain and used it as fuel. Because every time you change the story, even in small ways, you're breaking down the cage and turning it into something you can build on.

## Tip #2: Set Boundaries Like a Boss

Trauma can leave us with some pretty warped ideas about boundaries. Maybe you learned that saying "no" was dangerous, that keeping the peace was more important than protecting yourself. But if you want to turn trauma into a catalyst, you have to start setting boundaries that honor your worth and your needs. Boundaries are your way of saying, "I'm not willing to sacrifice myself to keep anyone else comfortable." They're a way of reclaiming control over your life, a declaration that you are not here to be walked over, minimized, or ignored.

Start small. Maybe it's saying "no" when someone asks for more than you can give. Maybe it's distancing yourself from people who don't respect you. Or maybe it's letting someone know that their behavior is unacceptable. Every time you set a boundary, you're reclaiming a piece of yourself. You're taking trauma and using it as a lesson in self-respect, in knowing what you will and won't tolerate. Boundaries aren't walls to keep everyone out; they're standards that make space for the people and things that support you.

## Tip #3: Focus on What You Can Control

One of the most paralyzing effects of trauma is the feeling that everything is out of your control. Trauma takes away your power; it makes you feel small, vulnerable, and at the mercy of forces you can't influence. But here's the reality: you have control over more than you think. You can't change the past, but you can choose how you respond to it. You can't make someone love you or treat you the way you deserve, but you can choose who you let into your life. By focusing on what you *can* control, you're turning trauma into a source of strength rather than a source of weakness.

Make a list. Write down everything in your life that you have control over, even the small things. Your routines, your habits, your goals, the people you surround yourself with—these are all things within your power. And every time you focus on them, every time you make a choice that aligns with who you want to be, you're reinforcing your resilience. Trauma doesn't get to dictate your choices anymore. You do.

## Tip #4: Create Your Own "Non-Negotiables"

Your non-negotiables are the standards you set for yourself that aren't up for debate. These are the things that, no matter what life throws at you, you refuse to compromise on. They're the values that trauma may have challenged but didn't destroy. Maybe it's honesty, loyalty, respect, or authenticity. Whatever it is, these non-negotiables become your compass, your guide for making decisions and building relationships.

For example, if one of your non-negotiables is respect, then anyone who disrespects you doesn't get a place in your life. If one of your values is authenticity, then you commit to showing up as your real self, even if it's uncomfortable. Trauma has a way of making us feel like we have to bend, to conform, to shrink. But when you establish non-negotiables, you're drawing a line. You're saying, "This is who I am, and I won't compromise it." These values become the building blocks for a life that isn't controlled by past hurts but driven by personal principles.

## Tip #5: Practice "Micro-Bravery"

Healing from trauma and breaking old patterns doesn't require you to take huge leaps all at once. In fact, sometimes the smallest steps are the most transformative. Micro-bravery is about those little moments where you do the opposite of what trauma taught you. It's about speaking up when your instinct is to stay silent. It's about reaching out to someone when you're tempted to isolate. It's about allowing yourself to feel joy even when a part of you feels you don't deserve it. These small acts of bravery add up, creating a ripple effect that transforms your life over time.

You don't have to wait until you're "healed" to start living a life that's yours. Every small step, every little act of courage is a way of breaking free from the cage of trauma. Micro-bravery is about proving to yourself, over and over, that you're capable of more than you think. And every time you choose to do something brave, no matter how small, you're turning your trauma into a catalyst, a force that pushes you forward rather than holding you back.

---

Each of these tips is a way of reclaiming control, of turning trauma into something that fuels your growth rather than your fear. This isn't about ignoring the past or pretending it didn't affect you—it's about using it as the foundation for a life that's truly yours. Trauma doesn't have to be a sentence. It can be the reason you build, the reason you rise, the reason you finally live a life that isn't defined by what happened to you but by what you chose to become.

Turning trauma into a catalyst is powerful, but to make it truly transformative, you need a shift in mindset—a redefinition of what trauma represents in your life. Trauma doesn't have to be a life sentence or a permanent identity; it can be a teacher, a motivator, a foundation for something stronger. This isn't about downplaying the impact of what happened, but about choosing to let it serve you rather than define you. Here's how to start redefining the role of trauma in your life and make it part of a story that belongs to you—not one that controls you.

## Tip #1: "I Own This"

The first step to redefining trauma is taking ownership of it—not ownership in the sense that you wanted it or deserved it, but ownership in the sense that it's *yours*. No one else can define what you've been through, and no one else can dictate how you should feel about it. This trauma is part of your story, and by claiming it as yours, you're taking back the power to decide what it means to you. When you own it, you stop letting others tell you how to "get over it" or "move on." Instead, you get to decide what role it plays in your life.

This shift means saying, "Yes, this happened to me. Yes, it hurt. But I get to decide what happens next." Trauma becomes part of your identity, but not in a way that diminishes you. It becomes a mark of your resilience, a testament to everything you've survived. And once you own it, it's no longer something that happened *to* you—it's something you carry with strength and purpose.

## Tip #2: Release the "Shoulds"

One of the biggest traps of trauma is the feeling that you "should" be over it, that you "should" feel a certain way, or that you "should" have done things differently. These "shoulds" are rooted in guilt, shame, and regret, and they keep you tied to a version of yourself that you've outgrown. Redefining trauma means letting go of the "shoulds" and embracing the reality of what happened without judgment. Trauma isn't about what you *should* have done or how you *should* feel—it's about acknowledging what is, what happened, and choosing to build forward from there.

When you catch yourself thinking, "I should be over this by now" or "I should have seen it coming," recognize that these thoughts don't serve you. Replace them with, "This is where I am, and that's okay." When you release the "shoulds," you're freeing yourself from expectations that were never realistic to begin with. You're giving yourself permission to feel and heal at your own pace, without the weight of external judgments.

## Tip #3: Use Trauma as Insight

Trauma has a way of showing us things about ourselves that we might not have seen otherwise. It reveals vulnerabilities, exposes patterns, and brings our deepest fears to the surface. Redefining trauma means looking at it as a source of insight, as something that has taught you about yourself, about others, and about what truly matters to you. Trauma doesn't just leave scars—it leaves wisdom, too, if you're willing to look for it.

Ask yourself: What did this experience teach me about what I want in life? What boundaries did it show me I need? What values did it reinforce? Maybe it taught you that you're stronger than you ever imagined, that you deserve respect, or that you're capable of surviving things you never thought possible. These insights become guideposts, markers that help you shape a life that honors what you've been through and respects what you need moving forward.

## Tip #4: Find Purpose in the Pain

This is one of the hardest shifts to make, but it's also one of the most powerful. Trauma, when left unchecked, can feel like senseless suffering. But when you find purpose in the pain—when you make the choice to let it inspire you, to let it connect you with others, to let it drive you—it stops being something that weighs you down and starts being something that pushes you forward. Finding purpose doesn't mean your trauma "happened for a reason," but it does mean that you're choosing to give it meaning.

Purpose can look different for everyone. For some, it's about helping others who've been through similar experiences. For others, it's about using their story to fuel their art, their work, their relationships. Maybe you decide that your purpose is to show others that healing is possible, or maybe it's to live a life that's full, that's joyful, despite what happened. Whatever purpose you choose, it becomes a way of turning trauma into something that serves you, something that adds to your life instead of subtracting from it.

## Tip #5: Practice Radical Acceptance

Radical acceptance is the art of saying, "This happened, and I accept it." It's not about condoning what happened, and it's definitely not about pretending it didn't hurt. Radical acceptance is simply the act of acknowledging reality as it is, without fighting it or wishing it away. When you accept your trauma as part of your story, as part of who you are, you stop resisting it, and in doing so, you free yourself to start building from there.

This doesn't mean you're okay with what happened. It just means you're done fighting against the fact that it happened. You're done wasting energy wishing things were different, and instead, you're focusing on what you can do from here. Radical acceptance is powerful because it shifts the focus from what's out of your control to what's within it. When you accept your trauma as part of your reality, you're giving yourself permission to stop looking back and to start looking forward.

## Tip #6: Create a Vision Beyond Trauma

It's easy to get stuck in the mindset that trauma is the defining point of your life, the thing that everything else revolves around. But redefining trauma means creating a vision of your life that goes beyond it. It means asking yourself, "Who do I want to be outside of this pain? What do I want my life to look like?" When you have a vision, you're giving yourself something to move toward. You're choosing to let trauma be part of your story, but not the whole story.

Creating a vision is about picturing the life you want, the person you want to be, the things that bring you joy and fulfillment. This vision doesn't erase the past, but it gives you a reason to keep moving forward. It reminds you that trauma is a chapter, not the whole book. And every time you take a step toward that vision, every time you make a choice that aligns with the life you want, you're breaking free from the limits trauma tried to place on you.

Redefining the role of trauma isn't about minimizing its impact or pretending it didn't hurt. It's about choosing to let it shape you in ways that make you stronger, more resilient, more aligned with the life you want to build. Trauma can be a cage, but it can also be a catalyst—one that pushes you to reclaim your story, to set new standards, to find purpose in places you never expected. Each of these shifts is a step toward making trauma part of your strength rather than a source of your pain.

# Chapter 4: Own the Hurt

It's time to talk about ownership—owning every scar, every painful memory, every wound that life has given you. We live in a world that wants us to hide our pain, to keep it buried and pretend it never happened. We're supposed to present this polished, unscarred version of ourselves to the world, as if vulnerability is something to be ashamed of. But here's the truth: **your scars are your strength**. Every wound you've survived, every piece of pain you've carried, is proof of your resilience. It's time to own it all unapologetically.

There's a power that comes from saying, "Yes, this is part of me." It's a power that the world doesn't understand because the world is used to pretending. But when you own your scars, when you claim them as part of who you are, you're refusing to let shame or fear control you. You're standing up and saying, "I am not defined by my pain, but I am not afraid to show it, either." Owning your hurt means integrating it into your identity in a way that empowers you, rather than weakens you. It means looking at every broken part of yourself and deciding that it's not a flaw—it's a badge of survival.

So how do you do that? How do you turn something that once tore you down into something that builds you up? It starts with changing the way you look at your pain. Society tells us that scars make us damaged goods, but that's a lie. Scars are signs of healing. They're proof that you've been through something that could've broken you, but instead, you're here. Scarred, yes, but standing. And standing with scars is more powerful than standing unmarked, because those scars show you're someone who doesn't just give up.

Here's a mindset shift to consider: **every wound you've survived is part of the reason you're as strong as you are today**. Each scar has taught you something, even if that lesson was hard-earned and painful. Maybe it taught you who you could trust, or maybe it taught you to rely on yourself. Maybe it forced you to dig deep and find strength you didn't know you had. Each experience, no matter how brutal, has added a layer to your resilience. And when you stop seeing those experiences as things to be ashamed of and start seeing them as sources of strength, you're reclaiming a part of yourself that trauma tried to take away.

This isn't about glorifying pain or pretending it doesn't hurt. It's about taking that pain and making it something that belongs to you, not something that controls you. Think of it like forging steel: the hottest fires create the strongest metal. And your pain, your scars, have been the fire. They've forged you into someone who's unbreakable, not because you haven't been hurt, but because you've learned how to carry that hurt without letting it define you.

There's a power in being able to show your scars and say, "Yes, I've been through hell, but I'm still here." It's a power that intimidates people who haven't faced their own pain, because it takes a hell of a lot more courage to own your hurt than to hide it. When you claim your scars, you're no longer hiding from them. You're no longer letting them dictate what you can and can't do. Instead, you're integrating them, making them part of your foundation, a source of strength rather than shame.

And there's another part of owning your hurt that's even more transformative: **when you own your pain, no one can use it against you**. When you're unapologetic about the things you've survived, you're taking the ammunition away from anyone who might try to use your past to put you down. You're showing them that you're not just unashamed—you're proud. Proud of everything you've survived, proud of every scar you carry, proud of the strength it took to make it through. When you own your hurt, you're bulletproof. You're unshakable, because you're no longer afraid of anyone finding out what you've been through. You've already claimed it as part of your story.

Owning your hurt is a radical act of self-acceptance. It's about looking at yourself, scars and all, and deciding that you're enough, exactly as you are. It's refusing to hide the parts of yourself that are "messy" or "damaged" because you know they're what make you real. And in a world that's obsessed with perfection, being real is a rebellion. It's standing tall in the face of everything that's tried to tear you down and saying, "I am still here, and I am not ashamed."

So, here's the first step: look at each scar, each painful memory, and decide that it's a source of strength, not a source of shame. Acknowledge that every experience, no matter how painful, has given you something. Maybe it's resilience, maybe it's empathy, maybe it's a clearer sense of what you want in life. Whatever it is, own it. Stop hiding from it, stop apologizing for it, and start letting it be a part of who you are—a part you're proud of.

Because here's the truth: the people who matter, the people who are meant to be part of your life, will respect you more for owning your scars. They'll see the strength it took to get here, the courage it takes to live openly and unapologetically, and they'll value you for it. And the people who can't handle it? They don't deserve a place in your story.

Own your hurt. Wear your scars. Let them be a testament to everything you've survived, a reminder of the strength it took to keep going. And remember that every scar is proof that you've made it through something that could've destroyed you. That's not something to hide—that's something to own with pride.

If you're like most people, you've probably spent a good chunk of your life hiding your pain. It's instinctive. Society tells us that emotions—especially the messy, painful ones—are best kept under wraps. We're conditioned to act like everything is fine, to keep our struggles behind closed doors. But here's the thing: hiding your pain doesn't make it go away. In fact, it does the opposite. Every time you shove it down, every time you mask it with a fake smile or pretend it didn't hurt, that pain festers. It grows, spreading like an infection. And before long, it's not just a hidden part of you—it becomes a constant drain on your energy, your spirit, and your sense of self.

Hiding your pain weakens you because it forces you to live a double life. On the outside, you're one version of yourself—the polished, put-together version that everyone expects to see. But on the inside, you're carrying all this unresolved pain, all these emotions that you never give yourself the chance to fully feel. It's exhausting, keeping those two lives separate. It takes a massive amount of energy to keep your pain hidden, to constantly keep up the act. And in the end, it leaves you feeling hollow, disconnected, and drained. When you're always pretending, you're robbing yourself of the chance to live authentically.

So why does visibility matter? Why is it so important to stop hiding and start letting your pain be seen? Because when you make your pain visible, you reclaim power over it. When you let people see your scars, you're saying, "This is part of me, and I'm not ashamed of it." Visibility is about taking ownership of your story instead of letting it control you in the shadows. When you let yourself be seen, scars and all, you're freeing yourself from the pressure to be perfect, to fit a mold that doesn't serve you. You're allowing yourself to be human—flawed, raw, and real.

There's a freedom in visibility. It's like stepping out of a cage you didn't even realize you were in. Suddenly, you're not constantly worrying about hiding parts of yourself, about covering up the things that make you feel vulnerable. You're just you, unapologetically. And that kind of authenticity, that refusal to pretend, is powerful. It attracts people who value honesty, who respect courage, and who want to connect on a level deeper than superficial small talk. Visibility lets you show up as your whole self, inviting others to do the same.

Let's also talk about the strength that comes from allowing yourself to be seen, especially when it's hard. When you hide your pain, you're telling yourself (even if it's subconscious) that there's something shameful about it. But when you make it visible, when you bring it into the light, you're taking control of the narrative. You're saying, "This is a part of my story, and I get to decide what it means." Instead of letting shame or fear dictate your life, you're choosing to embrace those scars as a part of your strength. Because here's the truth: people respect authenticity. They respect those who have been through hell and aren't afraid to show it.

Visibility also matters because it's how we find connection, real connection. When you let yourself be seen, you're opening the door for others to do the same. People who have been through their own struggles, who carry their own scars, will see you, and in you, they'll see permission to show their true selves. They'll find solidarity, the reassurance that they're not alone. When you're open about your pain, about the hard things you've faced, you create a space where others feel safe to be real, too. And that's how true connection is born—not from pretending everything is fine, but from showing up as you are and letting others do the same.

So what does visibility look like in practice? It doesn't mean oversharing or putting all your pain on display for the world. It means choosing to show your scars in a way that feels right for you. It might be telling a close friend about something you've been carrying alone. It might be sharing a piece of your story with someone who you know could benefit from hearing it. Or maybe it's as simple as allowing yourself to feel what you feel in the moment, without apologizing for it or trying to hide it. Visibility isn't about shouting your pain from the rooftops; it's about acknowledging that it's there and letting it be part of your truth.

Visibility is a form of self-respect. It's choosing to show up as the real, unfiltered version of yourself, even if that means some people might not understand or accept it. But here's the thing: the people who matter, the ones who truly value you, will see that strength and respect you for it. They'll recognize the courage it takes to live openly, to let yourself be seen. And the ones who don't? They were never meant to be part of your story anyway.

When you stop hiding, you start healing. You start living. You stop wasting energy on covering up the pain and start using it as part of the foundation for something real. You give yourself permission to be whole, scars and all. And in a world that's obsessed with appearances, that's a revolutionary act. Visibility isn't about needing everyone to know your story—it's about owning your story so fully that no one else's opinion can diminish it.

So, step into the light. Let your scars show. Let people see the strength it took to survive. You're not just a survivor—you're someone who has taken their pain, owned it, and turned it into a source of strength. And that's not something to hide. That's something to be proud of.

Loss, betrayal, anger—these are the kinds of experiences that leave marks. They're not the kinds of things that fade away easily or disappear with time. They're the kinds of experiences that, if you let them, can either break you or become the foundation of something stronger. If there's one thing I've learned from my own journey, it's this: the choice isn't in avoiding pain, because that's impossible. The choice is in what you do with it. And for me, that meant taking every hurt, every broken piece, and turning it into a part of my armor.

I've lived through enough loss to know that it doesn't get easier. Losing people, losing dreams, losing parts of yourself—each time, it takes a piece of you. But here's the thing: if you gather those pieces, if you don't let them scatter to the wind, they become something you can build with. For me, loss became a reminder that I could survive even the darkest days. When I lost my son, I thought it would destroy me. And in a way, it did; it shattered parts of me that I'll never get back. But in the wreckage, I found pieces of myself that were stronger, pieces that I didn't even know existed. I learned that as much as loss could take from me, it couldn't take everything. It couldn't take my resilience, my will to keep going. That loss became part of my armor, a part that reminds me every day that I've been through hell and come out on the other side.

Then there's betrayal—the kind of betrayal that cuts deep, that makes you question who you can trust, even makes you question yourself. Betrayal shakes your foundation, makes you feel like you're standing on ground that could give way at any second. But here's the thing about betrayal: as much as it hurts, it teaches you to set boundaries, to value yourself, and to protect your peace. Each time I was betrayed, I learned a little bit more about what I would and wouldn't tolerate, about the kind of people I wanted in my life. Betrayal taught me to draw lines, to respect myself enough to say, "I deserve better." And that, in itself, became another layer of my armor—a layer built on self-worth and a fierce commitment to never let anyone make me feel small or unworthy again.

And then there's anger, the kind of rage that builds when you've been wronged, abandoned, treated like you don't matter. Anger can be destructive, sure, but it can also be fuel. It's like a fire that can either burn you or propel you forward, depending on how you harness it. For years, I tried to bury my anger, thinking it was something shameful, something that would only make things worse. But what I realized is that anger is only toxic if you don't give it a purpose. When I started to own my anger, to let it remind me of the boundaries I needed to set, of the strength I needed to protect myself, it stopped being a weight and started being a source of energy. My anger became part of my armor because it reminded me that I'm not here to be walked on, that I have every right to stand up for myself, to defend my peace. Anger, when used with purpose, is powerful. It's the fuel that drives you to create a life that respects who you are and what you've been through.

Using pain as armor isn't about being invulnerable—it's about being resilient. It's about taking the pieces of yourself that have been hurt, scarred, or broken, and making them part of your strength. Loss, betrayal, anger—these aren't things to hide from; they're things to harness. Each one is a layer that makes you more whole, not less. They're reminders of everything you've survived, everything you've learned, everything you've become.

Here's an exercise that helped me: write down each major hurt, each betrayal, each loss. Take a moment with each one and ask yourself, "What did this teach me? What strength did this give me?" It might be hard to see it at first, but each of those experiences has left you with something. Maybe it's a better understanding of your own boundaries, maybe it's a sense of resilience, or maybe it's just the knowledge that you can survive even when it feels like you can't. Whatever it is, write it down. These aren't just memories; they're pieces of your armor. And when you start to see them as such, you stop seeing yourself as someone who's been damaged by life, and you start seeing yourself as someone who's been fortified by it.

Remember, your armor doesn't make you unbreakable—it makes you adaptable. It doesn't mean you'll never hurt again; it means you've learned to carry that hurt in a way that empowers you rather than weakens you. Each layer of armor is a reminder of what you've overcome, a declaration that, no matter how many times life tries to knock you down, you've learned how to rise.

So wear that armor. Let every scar, every wound, every painful memory be a testament to your strength. Because each one is proof that you're not just a survivor—you're someone who's taken life's hardest hits and come out stronger, someone who refuses to be defeated. And that's not just strength—that's power.

This is where we turn theory into practice. Owning your hurt is more than just saying you've been through some rough times; it's about actively reclaiming those experiences and seeing them through a new lens. It's about transforming your hurt story from one of helplessness into one of empowerment. And that's exactly what this exercise is designed to do. By writing your hurt story with a focus on resilience, growth, and strength, you'll start to see that your pain doesn't have to be a source of shame or regret—it can be your greatest source of power.

Here's how to do it. Set aside some time when you won't be interrupted. Grab a notebook, a pen, or whatever you use to write, and start by creating a space that feels comfortable and safe. This is a deep dive, and it's going to bring up a lot, so be ready to confront emotions that you might have buried. But remember, this isn't about dwelling on the past; it's about reframing it in a way that lets you see yourself not as a victim, but as someone who has survived, learned, and risen stronger.

## Step 1: Write the Raw Story

Start by writing out your hurt story exactly as it happened. Be raw, be real, and don't hold back. Write down the details, the emotions, the things you wish you could forget. Let yourself feel every part of it, even the pain that still lingers. This is the unfiltered version, the story as you remember it, without any reframing just yet. This part might feel heavy, and that's okay. You're bringing it all to the surface so that you can look at it fully, honestly. This is your truth, and there's power in speaking it without shame.

## Step 2: Identify the Strengths

Once you've written out your story, take a step back. Read through what you've written, but this time, look for moments of strength. Ask yourself: What did I learn from this experience? What did I survive that I didn't think I could? Where did I show resilience? Even in the worst moments, there are sparks of strength, decisions you made to keep going, things you did to protect yourself, to survive. Circle or highlight those parts. They're the proof that, even at your lowest, you had the strength to endure.

Look for the patterns too. Maybe you notice that, even though you felt powerless, you took actions that showed you were fighting for yourself. Or maybe you see that this experience taught you something about boundaries, about trust, about the value of self-respect. These are the parts of your story that show growth, that demonstrate that this hurt didn't destroy you—it shaped you.

## Step 3: Rewrite the Story with Power

Now, take what you've highlighted and start rewriting the story from a different perspective. Instead of focusing on what was done *to you*, focus on what you *did* in response. Rewrite it as the story of someone who faced incredible pain but didn't back down, someone who learned, who adapted, who grew. This isn't about erasing the hurt—it's about reclaiming it. Write this version of your story as if you're telling it to someone who needs to see you as the survivor, as the one who came out stronger. This is the version of your story that focuses on the power you found within yourself.

For example, if your original story was about betrayal and loss, this new version might focus on how you learned to set boundaries, how you built yourself back up, how you refused to let that betrayal define your worth. This is about taking back control over how your story is told. You're not ignoring the pain, but you're choosing to frame it in a way that highlights your strength, your resilience, your determination to keep going.

## Step 4: Declare Your Ownership

Finally, end this exercise by declaring that this is *your* story. It's yours to tell, yours to carry, and it belongs to no one else. Write a closing statement, something simple but powerful, that reclaims your pain as part of who you are. For example, "This story is mine. It's part of who I am, and I own every part of it." Or, "My hurt has shaped me, but it does not define me. I define myself." Say it out loud if you can. Feel the weight of it, feel the power in finally owning your story on your terms.

Owning your hurt doesn't mean the pain disappears; it means that the pain no longer controls you. This exercise is about taking those painful experiences, looking them in the face, and choosing to see them as part of the foundation that makes you who you are. It's about understanding that, no matter what happened, you are the author of your own life, and you get to decide how this story shapes you moving forward.

By claiming your hurt, by integrating it into your story as something that strengthens you rather than weakens you, you're building a kind of resilience that can't be shaken. This is what it means to own the hurt—to take everything you've survived and wear it as a mark of honor, as proof of your unbreakable spirit.

# Chapter 5: F*ck Their Opinions

If there's one thing that will drain your power faster than anything else, it's letting other people's opinions dictate your life. The problem is, we live in a society that's obsessed with image, with the need to impress, with fitting in and earning approval. From the moment we're old enough to understand, we're fed the idea that what other people think of us matters—that it's important, even essential, to live in a way that earns the validation of others. But here's the brutal truth: the opinions of others don't deserve to control your life. They don't deserve to steal your peace, your confidence, or your sense of self.

Other people's judgments are sneaky; they creep in through sideways glances, passing comments, or even silence. They make you question yourself, make you wonder if you're "too much" or "not enough." And if you let it, that doubt can take root, undermining every ounce of strength you've fought so hard to build. It's insidious, this pressure to conform, to fit into a box that wasn't made for you. But that pressure? It's poison. It's the quickest way to disconnect from who you really are, to lose sight of what you truly want.

Here's the thing about other people's opinions: they're rarely based on what's best for you. Instead, they're projections of other people's fears, insecurities, and limitations. When someone judges you, it's often because you're challenging something within them that they don't want to confront. Maybe your willingness to live openly makes them feel exposed, or your refusal to play by the rules makes them uncomfortable. Whatever the reason, their opinion has nothing to do with you—and everything to do with them.

Letting people's judgments guide your life is like handing them the keys and saying, "Here, you decide where I go." It's giving them power they don't deserve, power that should belong to you. Every time you make a choice based on what someone else might think, you're giving away a piece of your freedom. You're building your life on someone else's standards instead of your own. And that's no way to live.

So, how do you stop letting other people's opinions undermine your strength? First, you have to recognize that this need for approval runs deep, often so deep that we don't even realize it's there. It's that voice in the back of your head that questions whether you're making the "right" choice, not because it feels wrong to you, but because you're afraid of what others might say. It's that hesitation to speak your truth, to show up as yourself, because you're worried someone might disapprove.

The next step is to reframe those judgments. Whenever you feel the weight of someone else's opinion pressing down on you, ask yourself: *Who does this serve?* Does this judgment help you grow, help you get closer to the life you want, or does it just keep you small? Most of the time, you'll find that it doesn't serve you at all. It serves other people's expectations, other people's comfort zones. And the truth is, your life isn't here to make other people comfortable. Your life is here to be lived, fully and unapologetically, by you.

There's a freedom that comes with letting go of other people's judgments. It's the freedom to say, "This is who I am, and I'm not here to earn your approval." It's the freedom to make choices that feel right to you, regardless of whether anyone else understands or agrees. This doesn't mean you don't care about others; it means you care about yourself enough to live a life that's aligned with your own values, your own desires. It means choosing self-respect over approval.

People are always going to have opinions, and some of them will be negative. But here's a game-changer: their opinion isn't your problem. It's theirs. They can judge, they can disapprove, they can gossip—but none of that has to touch you. The moment you stop letting their opinions dictate your actions, you take back the power that's always been yours. You start living a life that's authentic, one that's built on your own choices, your own beliefs, and your own definition of success.

Here's a thought experiment: imagine a version of yourself that doesn't give a damn about what anyone else thinks. What choices would you make? What dreams would you chase? How would you show up in the world if the only approval you needed was your own? That version of you? That's the real you, the one that's been buried under layers of "shoulds" and expectations. That's the you that's waiting to be unleashed.

Living for yourself doesn't mean you're selfish; it means you're finally respecting yourself enough to live in alignment with who you are. It means acknowledging that you're the only one who has to live with your choices, so you're the only one who gets to make them. Other people's judgments are just noise, distractions from the path that's meant for you. So let them judge. Let them misunderstand. Let them have their opinions—and let them keep them.

Because at the end of the day, the opinions of others are temporary. They're fleeting, they're superficial, and they're irrelevant to the life you're building. But the respect you have for yourself? The pride you feel when you know you're living authentically? That's real. That's lasting. That's something no one can take from you.

So, you're ready to start living without the weight of other people's opinions holding you down. But how do you actually tune out the noise? In a world that's constantly telling you what to think, who to be, and how to live, going inward takes real discipline. It requires commitment, boundaries, and a willingness to sit with yourself, maybe even in the uncomfortable silence of your own thoughts. Here are some techniques to help you block out the noise, reconnect with your inner voice, and start building a life that's yours.

## Technique #1: The "Inner Circle" Filter

One of the most effective ways to tune out the opinions that don't serve you is to create an inner circle filter. Picture a small circle of people whose opinions truly matter to you. These are people who genuinely know you, who respect your values, and who care about your growth—not just about you fitting their expectations. When you're faced with decisions, criticisms, or doubts, ask yourself, "Is this coming from someone in my inner circle?" If it's not, then it's noise, plain and simple. It's feedback you don't need to internalize.

Your inner circle might be made up of close friends, a mentor, a partner, or even just your own gut instincts. If what you're hearing isn't coming from these sources, then you don't have to carry it. You can let it roll off, knowing that the only voices you're listening to are the ones that truly matter. And remember, the circle doesn't have to be big—quality over quantity. Most of the world's opinions are just filler. Let them float by without letting them stick.

## Technique #2: Practice Mindful Self-Check-Ins

It's easy to get swept up in other people's opinions, especially if you're not in the habit of checking in with yourself regularly. Mindful self-check-ins are a way to ground yourself, to reconnect with what you truly feel, and to distinguish between your own voice and the noise. Set aside a few minutes each day, whether it's in the morning, at night, or any quiet moment in between. During this time, ask yourself, "What do *I* think? What do *I* want? How do *I* feel?"

This might sound simple, but it's transformative. So much of our mental energy goes toward figuring out what others think or expect of us. But when you turn that energy inward, you start to develop a deeper sense of self-trust. You begin to recognize your own thoughts as distinct from everyone else's, and that's how you build the confidence to let go of external validation. Over time, these self-check-ins will become a habit, a way of life. You'll start naturally listening to yourself first, and the opinions of others will feel less relevant.

## Technique #3: Limit Social Media Exposure

Social media is a breeding ground for comparison, judgment, and unsolicited opinions. It's a place where people project their lives, their beliefs, their standards—usually without context or depth. If you want to tune out the noise, one of the best things you can do is set boundaries with social media. Limit your time on it, or take breaks altogether. Use it intentionally rather than passively. When you're on social media, remember that you're only seeing the highlight reels, the polished parts, the parts people want you to see. It's not reality, and it doesn't need to influence yours.

Unfollow or mute accounts that bring up feelings of inadequacy, judgment, or self-doubt. You're not obligated to absorb anyone's negativity or toxic messages. Curate your feed so that it aligns with your values, your goals, and your well-being. Social media is a tool, not a reflection of your worth. Treat it as such, and remember that you have the power to control what you see and what you allow to impact you.

## Technique #4: Set Personal Boundaries and Enforce Them

One of the quickest ways to lose yourself in others' opinions is by letting people overstep your boundaries. Set personal boundaries around what topics are open for discussion and what's off-limits. If someone tries to impose their beliefs, their judgments, or their unsolicited advice, politely let them know that their opinion isn't welcome on that matter. Boundaries aren't about pushing people away; they're about protecting your peace.

Maybe it's as simple as saying, "I appreciate your concern, but this is something I'm working through on my own." Or, "Thank you for your input, but I feel confident in my decision." When you set boundaries, you're reinforcing the message that your life is yours to live. You're showing people that while you respect their right to have an opinion, you're not here to entertain it. This might make some people uncomfortable, but those who respect you will respect your boundaries too.

## Technique #5: Visualize the Life You Want—Unfiltered

Take time to visualize the life you want in vivid detail. Imagine it as if no one else's opinions, expectations, or judgments mattered—because, in this exercise, they don't. Picture your ideal life as if it were entirely up to you (because, really, it is). Imagine your relationships, your work, your home, your daily routines. What do they look like? How do they feel? What does *authentic* happiness mean to you?

This kind of visualization is powerful because it's a reminder that your life is yours to shape. When you have a clear image of what you want, the opinions of others naturally hold less weight. You know where you're going, and their noise is just a distraction. Visualization gives you a destination, a goal, a clear direction. And when you're focused on what truly matters to you, the judgments of others lose their hold.

## Technique #6: Build a Habit of Self-Validation

This one takes practice, but it's essential: start validating yourself. Every time you make a choice that feels right for you, celebrate it. Acknowledge that you're making decisions that align with your own values, not someone else's. When you feel proud of yourself, give yourself credit. When you accomplish something, even if it's small, take a moment to feel good about it. Self-validation is about learning to give yourself the approval you've been looking for in others.

The more you validate yourself, the less you'll need it from anyone else. You'll build an inner resilience, a core of self-assurance that no one else can shake. When you know that you're proud of yourself, that you're making choices that align with who you are, other people's opinions will start to feel like background noise. This is your life, your journey, and no one else's approval is required.

These techniques aren't about isolating yourself from everyone's feedback; they're about choosing what feedback is worth listening to. They're about cultivating a strong sense of self, so that when other people's opinions inevitably come your way, they don't shake you. You get to decide what's important, what's meaningful, and what deserves your attention. The rest? Let it go. Let it drift by without clinging to it, and keep your focus inward, where the only opinion that truly matters resides—yours.

Building confidence that isn't swayed by other people's judgments starts with grounding yourself in your own values and priorities. It's about knowing, deep down, that who you are and what you believe in are enough. When your confidence comes from within, it becomes a foundation that can't be easily shaken by someone else's opinions. These exercises are designed to help you reconnect with your own values and build a rock-solid confidence that's rooted in who you are, not who anyone else thinks you should be.

## Exercise #1: Define Your Core Values

If you want to live confidently, you first have to know what matters to you. Grab a notebook and write down the values that are non-negotiable in your life—the things that you want your life to be built on, the principles that guide you. These might include honesty, independence, kindness, resilience, creativity—whatever feels right to you. There are no right or wrong answers here; this is about defining the values that align with your authentic self.

Once you've listed your values, rank them in order of importance. This will help you clarify which ones are most central to who you are. Then, reflect on how these values show up in your life. Are you living in alignment with them, or are there areas where you're compromising to please others? When you're clear on your values, you have a compass that can guide every decision you make. Other people's opinions will start to matter less because you'll know you're living a life that's true to you.

## Exercise #2: Create Your "Confidence Anchors"

A confidence anchor is something you can mentally or physically return to when self-doubt creeps in. It's a reminder of your strengths, achievements, and the reasons you can trust yourself. To create your confidence anchors, make a list of moments when you felt proud, resilient, or accomplished. These can be big or small—maybe it's something as significant as overcoming a major obstacle or as simple as standing up for yourself in a situation where it would've been easier to stay silent.

Once you've listed these moments, choose a few that resonate the most. These are your confidence anchors. Write them down, and refer to them whenever you feel yourself being swayed by someone else's opinion or doubting your worth. You can even create physical reminders, like a journal entry, a note on your phone, or a symbol you carry with you. The goal is to remind yourself that you have faced challenges, made difficult decisions, and that you're capable of handling whatever comes your way. Confidence isn't about being perfect; it's about trusting that you have the resilience to stand by who you are.

## Exercise #3: Write Your "Unapologetic Self" Declaration

Living unapologetically starts with declaring who you are and owning it fully. In this exercise, you'll write a declaration of your true self—your values, your beliefs, your passions, and the things you refuse to compromise on. This isn't for anyone else; it's for you. Start with "I am..." and let the words flow. Write about who you are without filtering, without apologizing, without worrying about anyone else's opinions.

For example: "I am resilient. I value honesty and authenticity above all else. I am creative, unapologetically myself, and I live by my own rules. I am proud of my scars and the journey they represent. I am here to live for me, not for anyone else's standards." Let this be your manifesto. When you feel uncertain or start to question yourself, read it as a reminder of who you are, on your terms. This declaration isn't set in stone—it can evolve with you as you grow. But having a written reminder of your core self is powerful. It's a way of grounding yourself in your truth whenever the world tries to pull you away from it.

## Exercise #4: Practice "Boundary Affirmations"

Setting boundaries is one of the strongest ways to protect your confidence and keep other people's judgments from affecting you. But boundaries can feel challenging, especially if you're used to putting others first. To strengthen your resolve, create a list of boundary affirmations that reinforce the importance of protecting your energy, time, and well-being. These affirmations should be personal and aligned with your core values.

Some examples:

- "I have the right to say no without feeling guilty."
- "My time and energy are valuable, and I choose where to invest them."
- "I am allowed to set boundaries that protect my mental and emotional health."
- "I do not owe anyone an explanation for living my life in a way that aligns with my values."

Repeat these affirmations to yourself daily, especially when you feel pressured to prioritize others' opinions over your own needs. Over time, these affirmations will help you build the confidence to set boundaries without hesitation. They reinforce the idea that your life is yours to shape and that setting limits isn't selfish—it's necessary.

## Exercise #5: Visualize Your Confident Self

Visualization is a powerful tool for building confidence because it helps you imagine and feel the emotions you want to experience. Close your eyes and picture the most confident version of yourself. Imagine yourself standing tall, radiating self-assurance, and making choices without fear of judgment. Picture yourself handling criticism calmly, setting boundaries with ease, and staying true to your values, no matter what others think.

Visualize a day in your life as this confident version of yourself. See yourself moving through situations where you might normally feel self-doubt or pressure, but instead, you stand firm, centered in your sense of self. Imagine how good it feels to be fully in control of your decisions, knowing that you're living for yourself, not for anyone else's approval. Do this visualization regularly, especially when you're feeling low on confidence. The more vividly you can picture it, the more you'll start to embody it in your daily life.

**Exercise #6: Write a "Confidence Journal"**

In a notebook or document, create a confidence journal. Each day, write down one thing you did that aligned with your values or one decision you made that prioritized your own voice over others' opinions. These can be big things, like setting a firm boundary, or small things, like choosing an activity that you enjoy without worrying about what others think.

By keeping track of these moments, you'll start to see your confidence growing. You'll have a record of the ways you're stepping into your own power, even when it feels challenging. And on days when self-doubt creeps in, you can look back and see all the times you stood by yourself, proving that you're capable of living in alignment with who you are.

---

Each of these exercises is designed to reinforce the idea that your confidence is yours to build, not something that depends on anyone else's validation. These practices help ground you in your own values, anchor you in your own strength, and give you tools to keep other people's opinions from derailing your self-worth. Over time, as you commit to living by your own standards, you'll find that confidence becomes less about what anyone else thinks and more about knowing, deeply, that you're exactly where you're meant to be—living as unapologetically you.

Letting go of the need for other people's approval is like shedding a weight you didn't even realize you were carrying. Once it's gone, you feel lighter, freer. It's as if you've been holding your breath for years, and finally, you get to exhale. When you stop caring about what others think, you start living for yourself, making choices that align with your own needs, your own dreams, your own truth. And that kind of freedom? It's rare, it's precious, and it's transformative.

The first change you'll notice is a sense of peace. When you let go of external validation, you're no longer spending your energy on constantly monitoring yourself, adjusting your behavior, or censoring your words to fit into someone else's idea of who you should be. You're no longer playing a role or trying to be liked by people who may never fully understand you. Instead, you're focused inward, grounded in your own sense of purpose, and that's where true peace begins. You stop running, you stop pretending, and for the first time, you're able to just be.

Another powerful shift? The people in your life start to change. When you're living authentically, you're no longer attracting people who only like the edited version of you. Instead, you're drawing in people who appreciate you as you are—people who respect your boundaries, who value your honesty, who encourage your growth. And as for the people who can't handle the real you? They'll either distance themselves or make their disapproval known, but you'll find that you're okay with that. You don't need them to get it. The people who are meant to be in your life are the ones who celebrate your authenticity, not the ones who try to mold you into their version of "acceptable."

Letting go of other people's opinions also brings a newfound confidence. You start to feel more comfortable taking risks, going after goals that you might have once dismissed as "too out there" or "too risky." When you're no longer afraid of failure in the eyes of others, you're free to explore, to experiment, to pursue the things that light you up without worrying about how it'll look to anyone else. You learn to see setbacks as part of the journey, not as something to be ashamed of. You find yourself embracing the process, not just the end result, and that makes everything richer, more fulfilling.

There's a deep resilience that comes with this freedom. When your worth is rooted in your own beliefs rather than in someone else's approval, criticism and rejection lose their sting. Sure, it's human to feel hurt sometimes, but it no longer derails you. It doesn't shake your core, because your core isn't built on shaky foundations of other people's opinions—it's built on your own strength, your own integrity, your own values. You learn to see criticism as feedback, not a reflection of your worth. You get to decide what's constructive and worth listening to, and what's just noise to let go.

This freedom also allows you to be kinder—to yourself and to others. When you're no longer focused on living up to someone else's standards, you stop judging yourself so harshly, and in turn, you stop judging others as well. You become more accepting, more understanding, because you know what it feels like to reject the pressure of perfection. You recognize that everyone is on their own path, and just as you're choosing to live freely, you allow others to do the same.

Letting go of external approval doesn't mean you live in isolation. It means you're able to connect with people from a place of authenticity rather than fear. You're not looking for validation; you're looking for genuine connection. And the connections that come from this place are stronger, deeper, and real. You find yourself surrounded by people who see you, who truly value you, who don't expect you to be anything other than who you are. And that's where true belonging happens—not in fitting in, but in finding a place where you're accepted as you are.

So here's the ultimate freedom: when you stop living for other people's approval, you start living for yourself. You give yourself permission to pursue what matters to you, to be bold, to take up space, to embrace your quirks, to honor your needs. You stop apologizing for being who you are, and instead, you start celebrating it. And in a world that's always trying to tell you to fit in, to be smaller, to conform, that's the most powerful thing you can do.

# Chapter 6: The Power of Being Real

Authenticity is one of the rarest things in the world, yet it's the one quality that makes us feel the most alive, the most whole. Being real—truly, unapologetically real—is a radical act, especially in a world that encourages us to mask our true selves and present a polished, "acceptable" version instead. But authenticity isn't just about being transparent; it's the foundation of self-respect, of inner strength, and of a life that feels aligned with who you really are.

When you choose authenticity, you're choosing self-respect over approval. You're choosing to be true to your values, your beliefs, and your needs, even if it makes some people uncomfortable. Being real means you're willing to stand by your choices, not because they're popular, but because they feel right to you. And this choice, this commitment to being authentic, builds a kind of self-respect that no external approval can ever match. Because at the end of the day, it's not about who accepts you—it's about whether you accept yourself.

Here's the truth: authenticity isn't always easy. It's going to ruffle feathers, challenge expectations, and occasionally make you feel like you're standing alone. But the flip side? There's a strength in being real that no one can take away. When you're unapologetically yourself, you're creating a foundation that can't be shaken by judgment, rejection, or criticism. You're building your life on solid ground, rooted in who you are rather than in who anyone else wants you to be. And that kind of foundation? It's unbreakable.

Authenticity is also freeing. When you stop pretending, you release the weight of trying to be someone you're not. You stop second-guessing yourself, worrying about what people might think, or adjusting your personality to fit into someone else's version of "acceptable." Being real gives you permission to show up as you are—unfiltered, unpolished, and fully human. And in that freedom, you find a sense of peace that can't be replicated. Because when you're real, you're finally living in alignment with yourself, not with anyone else's expectations.

Living authentically doesn't mean you won't feel fear or self-doubt. It just means you won't let those feelings steer your life. You might hesitate before speaking your truth, worry about how others will respond, or feel vulnerable in moments of honesty. But instead of letting those fears keep you small, you let them become part of the process. Authenticity isn't about being fearless—it's about being courageous enough to be real, even when it's uncomfortable.

Here's the thing: when you're authentic, you're setting an example for others to do the same. Your honesty, your willingness to show up as you are, gives other people permission to do the same. It's a reminder that they don't have to hide their flaws or mask their feelings to be accepted. This doesn't mean everyone will like it; some people will find your authenticity intimidating, even confrontational, because it challenges them to look at the ways they might be hiding. But for others, your authenticity will be a breath of fresh air, a reminder that real connection happens when people show up as themselves.

Authenticity is the foundation of true connection. When you're real, the people who resonate with who you truly are will naturally gravitate toward you. The ones who don't? They'll fall away, and that's okay. Authenticity filters out the noise, leaving you with relationships that are built on mutual respect, shared values, and a deep understanding of each other's truths. You're no longer playing a role or guessing what people want to see—you're just being yourself, and that's enough.

Finally, being real creates a foundation of strength that no external force can shake. Because when your life is built on authenticity, you don't need anyone else's approval to feel validated. Your worth doesn't come from what you do, how you look, or how well you fit into other people's expectations. It comes from knowing that you're living a life that aligns with who you are. And that kind of confidence, that unshakable inner strength, is priceless.

So here's the bottom line: authenticity is more than just a choice—it's a lifestyle. It's deciding every day to show up as yourself, even when it's easier to conform, even when it feels vulnerable, even when people don't understand. Because at the end of the day, the only opinion that truly matters is your own. And when you're living authentically, that opinion is one you can be proud of.

One of the biggest benefits of living authentically is the resilience it builds. Authenticity and resilience are deeply connected because when you're real with yourself—about who you are, what you want, and what matters most—you have a foundation that can weather life's storms. Living authentically doesn't mean life will be easy or that you'll avoid hardship, but it means you'll face those challenges grounded in a truth that belongs entirely to you.

Here's why authenticity is such a powerful source of resilience: when you're committed to being true to yourself, you're better equipped to handle what life throws at you. You're not constantly bending or breaking to meet other people's expectations. You're not trying to keep up with a facade or play a role that's exhausting to maintain. Instead, you're standing strong in your values, knowing that no matter how hard things get, you have a core self to rely on.

Consider this: when you're living for approval or adapting yourself to please others, every criticism, every setback, and every moment of failure feels like a hit to your identity. Because if your sense of self-worth is tied up in what others think, then any time someone disapproves or doubts you, it can shake your entire foundation. But when you're authentic—when your identity is rooted in your own values, your own truth—those external judgments don't carry the same weight. Criticism becomes feedback rather than a threat. Challenges become learning experiences rather than failures. You're able to bounce back because you're not looking to others for validation; you're looking within.

Another way authenticity builds resilience is by giving you permission to fail. When you're real with yourself, you stop expecting perfection. You accept that failure, mistakes, and setbacks are part of the journey. You learn to see them not as reflections of your worth but as stepping stones that contribute to your growth. Authenticity allows you to fail without losing yourself in the process, to make mistakes without spiraling into self-doubt. Because at the end of the day, you know who you are, flaws and all, and you know that your worth doesn't depend on getting everything right.

Living authentically also creates resilience through deeper connections. When you're real, you attract people who genuinely support you, who see you for who you are and love you without conditions. These connections become a source of strength during hard times. They're the people you can turn to without fear of judgment, the ones who encourage you to stay true to yourself, who remind you of your worth when life makes you question it. This kind of support network is invaluable because it's built on mutual trust, respect, and understanding. And having people like that in your corner strengthens your ability to face whatever comes your way.

There's also a unique type of resilience that comes from self-acceptance—the kind that can only come when you're being true to yourself. When you're authentic, you're not hiding from your weaknesses, your insecurities, or your past. You accept these parts of yourself, and in doing so, they lose their power to control you. You become resilient because you're no longer fighting against who you are or running from parts of your story. You embrace them, even the painful parts, knowing that they contribute to the whole of who you are. This level of self-acceptance is what allows you to stand firm when life tests you. It's what gives you the courage to keep going, even when the path is rough.

Being real is about having the courage to live a life that's true, not easy. And resilience is born from that courage. It's built through the times when you stay true to yourself despite pressure, when you choose authenticity over approval, when you make decisions that reflect your values rather than others' expectations. Each time you do this, you're strengthening your inner resolve, building a foundation that can handle life's uncertainties because it's rooted in something unshakeable: the real you.

So here's the truth: authenticity makes you resilient because it gives you the freedom to live on your own terms. It allows you to face life's toughest moments without losing yourself, without compromising your core values, and without sacrificing your self-worth. When you're real, you're free. And when you're free, you're strong enough to face anything.

Living authentically isn't something you just decide to do overnight; it's a habit, a skill that takes time to build and refine. Every day, you have choices that bring you closer to living as your true self or further from it. These exercises are designed to help you tune into your authentic self, to let go of habits that encourage conformity, and to cultivate a life that reflects who you are, not who the world expects you to be.

### Exercise #1: Daily "Check-In" Ritual

A big part of living authentically is knowing how you feel and what you want—without being influenced by other people's opinions or expectations. Set aside five to ten minutes each day for a personal check-in. You can do this in the morning to set the tone for the day or in the evening to reflect on how things went.

Ask yourself:

- "What am I feeling today?"
- "What's important to me right now?"
- "Is there anything I did today that didn't align with who I am or what I value?"

This simple check-in ritual builds self-awareness, helping you notice when you're acting in ways that don't align with your true self. The more you practice, the more you'll start catching yourself in moments of inauthenticity, allowing you to make choices that reflect your true self.

Exercise #2: Identify and Challenge "Should" Statements

"Should" statements are a sign that you're letting external expectations dictate your actions. Anytime you find yourself thinking, "I should be doing this," or "I should want that," take a pause and examine where it's coming from. Ask yourself:

- "Who says I should do this?"
- "Is this something I truly want, or am I doing it to fit into someone else's standards?"
- "What would I do if I didn't care what others thought?"

The goal is to start replacing "should" with "want" or "need." Instead of thinking, "I should go to this event," reframe it as, "Do I *want* to go, or do I feel obligated?" Each time you do this, you're strengthening your ability to choose actions that align with your authentic desires rather than someone else's expectations.

## Exercise #3: "No Apologies" Journal

Get a journal where you can be completely unfiltered—no apologies, no editing, no censoring. Write down your thoughts, emotions, and opinions, exactly as they are. This journal is your safe space to express everything you feel without worrying about how it will be received.

Write about what frustrates you, excites you, scares you, and makes you feel alive. Describe your dreams, your desires, your ambitions, no matter how big or unconventional they may be. The point is to let go of the need to filter yourself for others. The more you practice being unapologetically real with yourself, the easier it becomes to show up authentically in the world.

## Exercise #4: Act from Your "Future Self" Perspective

Think of the most authentic version of yourself—the version that's bold, honest, and true to their own values. Imagine this version of you ten years from now. Ask yourself, "What choices would my future self make?" or "How would my future self handle this situation?"

By looking at your decisions through the lens of your future self, you're more likely to act in alignment with your true values. You're not thinking about what's easy in the moment or what will keep everyone happy; you're thinking about what's right for the long haul. Acting from your future self's perspective is a powerful way to build a life that's grounded in authenticity.

## Exercise #5: Define and Uphold Your "Non-Negotiables"

Non-negotiables are boundaries or values that you refuse to compromise on, no matter the situation. These might include honesty, respect, creativity, or time for self-care. Write down your non-negotiables and keep them somewhere visible as a daily reminder.

Each time you face a decision, check it against your non-negotiables. Ask yourself, "Does this align with my core values? Does this respect my boundaries?" By clearly defining and upholding your non-negotiables, you're sending a message to yourself and the world that you're committed to living a life that honors who you are.

## Exercise #6: The "True Self" Filter for Relationships

When we're not living authentically, we often find ourselves in relationships (whether friends, family, or partners) that require us to conform or compromise our true selves. Take a close look at your relationships and ask yourself:

- **"Do I feel like I can be my full self with this person?"**
- **"Does this relationship encourage or suppress my authenticity?"**
- **"Am I respected for who I am, or am I expected to be someone I'm not?"**

If you find that a relationship consistently demands you to hide or compromise your true self, it might be worth reevaluating. Authenticity in relationships is a two-way street. You deserve to be around people who respect your truth, just as they deserve someone who respects theirs. Use this filter to refine your connections and build relationships that support your growth, not ones that hold you back.

---

These exercises aren't about changing who you are; they're about uncovering the real you. Authenticity is a muscle, and each time you choose to act in alignment with your true self, that muscle gets stronger. The goal here isn't perfection—there will always be times when you slip into old patterns or let fear sway your choices. But with each step, each choice that aligns with who you really are, you're building a life that feels more genuine, more free, and more deeply connected to your own truth.

Living authentically isn't a one-time decision; it's a commitment. In a world that constantly encourages us to conform, showing up as yourself takes courage, resilience, and a willingness to stand out. But once you taste the freedom of being real, it's hard to go back to hiding, pretending, or shrinking yourself to fit in. Authenticity brings a level of freedom that's unlike anything else—freedom from pretending, from needing approval, from doubting yourself every time you make a choice. And that freedom? It's worth fighting for.

The beauty of embracing true self-expression is that it's liberating not only for you but also for the people around you. When you show up authentically, you give others permission to do the same. It's as if your presence sends a message that it's okay to be real, that it's okay to let go of the act and just be. This kind of authenticity is contagious, and it can transform your relationships, your work, and your sense of purpose. But to keep this freedom alive, especially in a world that encourages conformity, you have to practice self-expression intentionally.

So, how do you keep showing up authentically, day after day, even when it feels easier to blend in? Here's how.

## Tip #1: Create Your Own "Permission Slips"

Sometimes, you just need to give yourself permission to be real. Write down a few permission slips for yourself that encourage authenticity. They might look something like:

- "I give myself permission to say no without feeling guilty."
- "I give myself permission to express my feelings, even if they're uncomfortable for others."
- "I give myself permission to prioritize my own needs."
- "I give myself permission to be imperfect and still worthy."

Whenever you feel that urge to conform or to hold back, pull out one of these permission slips. Remind yourself that you don't need anyone else's approval to show up as your true self. This simple practice can help you stand firm in moments of doubt and reinforce that you are allowed to live on your terms.

## Tip #2: Celebrate Your Quirks

Authenticity isn't about fitting into a mold; it's about celebrating what makes you unique. Start embracing your quirks, the things that make you stand out, even if they're not "normal" or mainstream. Maybe you have an unusual laugh, a deep passion for a hobby that others don't understand, or a way of seeing the world that feels different from the norm. Rather than hiding these parts, bring them forward. They're what make you, *you*.

When you celebrate your quirks, you're reinforcing the message that you're proud of who you are, not embarrassed by it. And the more you lean into those unique aspects, the more comfortable you'll feel being unapologetically yourself.

## Tip #3: Speak Up When It Matters

Part of being authentic is speaking up for what you believe in, even when it's easier to stay silent. This doesn't mean you have to voice every opinion or get involved in every debate. It simply means that, when something truly matters to you, you honor that feeling by expressing it. Speaking up can be intimidating, especially if you're used to keeping your thoughts to yourself. But each time you choose to speak your truth, you're strengthening your authenticity muscle.

Start with small moments—a comment during a conversation, an opinion you usually keep to yourself, a gentle disagreement. The more you practice, the easier it becomes to express your views in a way that feels natural, not forced. And over time, this builds confidence, making it easier to stand up for your values and beliefs in larger, more impactful ways.

## Tip #4: Practice Saying "No" Without Explanation

One of the biggest challenges to living authentically is the pressure to please others. Saying no can feel like you're letting people down, but it's actually one of the most powerful ways to honor your true self. Start practicing saying "no" without offering an explanation. This might feel uncomfortable at first, but it's a reminder that you don't owe anyone a reason for choosing what's right for you.

Instead of saying, "I can't because I have to do something else," try simply saying, "No, thank you." Or, "That doesn't work for me." Each time you say no without feeling the need to justify it, you're reinforcing that your choices don't need to be validated by anyone else. You're reclaiming your time, your energy, and your boundaries. And each time you do this, you're taking a stand for your authentic self.

## Tip #5: Surround Yourself with Authentic People

The people around you have a huge impact on your ability to live authentically. Seek out relationships with people who value honesty, who aren't afraid to be vulnerable, and who encourage you to be real. These are the people who will remind you of your worth when you start to doubt it, who will challenge you to stay true to yourself, and who will celebrate your growth rather than trying to hold you back.

Authentic connections create a safe space for self-expression. When you're surrounded by people who live genuinely, it becomes easier to do the same. You'll find yourself opening up more, trusting more, and feeling more confident in showing up as you are. These relationships become a source of strength, reminding you that you're not alone in your journey toward authenticity.

## Tip #6: Reflect Regularly on Your Journey

Living authentically is a journey, not a destination. Regularly take time to reflect on where you are in that journey. Ask yourself:

- "Am I showing up as my true self in my relationships, my work, my daily life?"
- "Are there any areas where I'm holding back or trying to fit in?"
- "What's one step I can take today to be more aligned with my authentic self?"

These reflections don't have to be long or formal. They're just check-ins to keep you connected with your core self, to keep you grounded in your values, and to ensure that you're living in alignment with the life you want to build. When you make reflection a habit, you become more attuned to moments when you're straying from your truth, allowing you to correct course and keep moving forward authentically.

---

Living authentically is a lifelong practice, a series of choices that reaffirm who you are and what you stand for. And while it might feel challenging at times, the freedom that comes from being real is worth every bit of effort. You're here to live your life—not anyone else's version of it. And the more you show up as your true self, the more you'll find that the world meets you there, bringing people, opportunities, and experiences that resonate with who you truly are.

So embrace the freedom of being real. Keep choosing authenticity, keep showing up as yourself, and keep reminding yourself that you're enough exactly as you are. Because that's the power of being real: it sets you free to live a life that's truly, unapologetically, yours.

# Chapter 7: Embrace the Pain

Pain has a way of sticking around, of lingering in the background, until you face it head-on. We're taught to avoid it, to cover it up, to move past it as quickly as possible. Society tells us that feeling pain is a sign of weakness, something to be ignored or numbed. But here's the truth that no one likes to admit: avoiding pain doesn't make it go away; it makes it stronger. When you ignore or suppress it, that pain doesn't vanish—it festers, growing heavier and more intense over time. It becomes the weight you carry, the shadow that follows you, the underlying tension that creeps into every part of your life.

The reality is that pain demands to be felt. The more you avoid it, the more it asserts itself, finding ways to seep into your thoughts, your relationships, your decisions. It influences how you see yourself and how you engage with the world around you. Avoidance doesn't make pain disappear; it just delays the inevitable. And the longer you wait, the harder it becomes to confront. Pain, when ignored, doesn't stay stagnant—it gains momentum, finding ways to remind you it's still there, whether that's through stress, anxiety, or feeling numb to life altogether.

Facing pain is terrifying, no doubt. It means sitting with the discomfort, feeling the things you've been trying to escape, and letting yourself experience emotions that you might have buried for years. But here's the thing: when you confront pain instead of running from it, you take back control. Pain loses its grip because it's no longer something you're afraid of; it's something you're actively working through. You're no longer its prisoner. By choosing to feel it, you're acknowledging its presence, accepting that it's part of your experience, and, most importantly, allowing yourself to heal.

Embracing pain isn't about wallowing or getting stuck in it. It's about processing it so that you can move forward, so that you can release its hold on you. When you allow yourself to feel the sadness, the anger, the disappointment, you're giving those emotions a space to exist, which is the first step toward letting them go. Pain needs to be felt in order to be released. It's a paradox, but the only way to lessen its power is to lean into it, to let it wash over you, and to trust that you can survive it.

This doesn't mean you'll feel better instantly. Embracing pain is a process. It requires patience, self-compassion, and the willingness to be vulnerable. But as you sit with your pain, as you let yourself feel it fully, you'll find that its intensity starts to diminish. You begin to understand it better, to see what it's trying to tell you. Maybe it's revealing unmet needs, unresolved wounds, or areas in your life that need attention. Pain, when acknowledged, becomes a teacher rather than a burden. It becomes a source of insight, helping you understand yourself more deeply and showing you where healing needs to happen.

The freedom that comes from embracing pain is profound. You stop being afraid of the hard moments, the emotional lows, the times when life doesn't go as planned. Instead, you learn to trust yourself to handle them. You build resilience, a strength that comes from knowing you can face anything, that no feeling is too overwhelming, no experience too painful for you to survive. This resilience becomes a part of you, giving you the courage to live more fully, to take risks, to open yourself up to new experiences without the fear of being hurt.

Here's the bottom line: avoiding pain keeps you stuck, but embracing it sets you free. The sooner you confront it, the sooner you can heal, the sooner you can move forward. Pain isn't something to be ashamed of; it's part of being human. And by choosing to feel it rather than run from it, you're choosing growth, strength, and ultimately, freedom.

Pain is one of life's greatest teachers, though it rarely feels that way when you're in the middle of it. When you're hurting, it's hard to see anything beyond the immediate discomfort, the weight of the emotions, the heaviness that seems to settle in your chest. But if you're willing to look deeper, pain can teach you things that comfort never will. There's a strength, a depth, and a wisdom that only comes from surviving hard things. And when you learn to let pain be a teacher, it transforms from something that breaks you into something that builds you.

The first lesson pain offers is resilience. Every time you go through something difficult and come out on the other side, you're proving to yourself that you can survive, that you're stronger than you think. Pain shows you that you have the ability to endure, even when it feels impossible. Each painful experience adds another layer of resilience, making you better equipped to handle whatever comes next. You learn to trust yourself, to rely on your own strength, because you know you've survived before, and you'll survive again.

Pain also teaches you empathy. When you've been through suffering, you gain a level of understanding for others who are hurting. You know what it feels like to be low, to feel isolated, to question yourself, and that experience allows you to connect with others on a deeper level. Empathy is born from shared pain, from the understanding that life is hard and that everyone has their own battles. This empathy becomes a source of connection, allowing you to offer support, kindness, and compassion to others, often when they need it most. Pain makes you more human, more relatable, and ultimately, more open to the experiences of others.

Another lesson in pain is self-awareness. Pain has a way of revealing things about yourself that you might not have noticed otherwise. It forces you to examine your beliefs, your patterns, and your choices. Maybe you realize you've been tolerating less than you deserve, or maybe you see that you've been ignoring parts of yourself that need attention. Pain makes you stop, take a step back, and look inward. It invites you to question what's working, what's not, and where you need to make changes. Pain has a brutal honesty to it—it shows you what you can't ignore, what you need to address, and where growth needs to happen.

Pain can also teach you the value of boundaries. Often, the hardest lessons in pain come from situations where we allowed ourselves to be mistreated, ignored our intuition, or compromised our values. Pain shows you where you need to protect yourself, where you need to set limits, and where you need to walk away. It teaches you that not everyone deserves access to your energy, your time, or your heart. Boundaries aren't about closing yourself off—they're about respecting yourself enough to guard what's valuable. When you learn to let pain guide your boundaries, you're no longer willing to settle for situations or people that don't honor your worth.

Finally, pain teaches you the importance of letting go. There's a unique kind of freedom that comes from releasing what no longer serves you, from letting go of the past, of resentments, of unmet expectations. Pain teaches you that holding onto things that hurt only prolongs your suffering. By letting go, you're choosing to make space for healing, for growth, for new experiences. Letting go doesn't mean you forget what happened or that the pain didn't matter—it means you're choosing not to let it control your future. You're reclaiming your power by releasing the weight that's been holding you down.

Letting pain make you stronger is about accepting that suffering is a part of life, but it doesn't have to define you. Every time you choose to find the lesson in pain, every time you let it teach you rather than break you, you're building a foundation of resilience, empathy, self-awareness, and wisdom. You're choosing to let pain shape you in ways that make you better, not bitter. This is what it means to embrace the pain—to look it in the face, to feel it fully, and to use it as fuel for growth.

So the next time you're faced with something difficult, ask yourself, "What can this pain teach me? How can I use it to become stronger, wiser, more grounded in who I am?" Pain isn't just something to survive; it's something to learn from, something to grow through. And when you let pain make you stronger, you're transforming it from a source of suffering into a source of power.

Pain is uncomfortable, messy, and overwhelming. That's why most of us try to avoid it, pushing it down or distracting ourselves so we don't have to feel it. But avoiding pain only delays healing. It keeps you stuck, turning it into something you carry long after the initial hurt has passed. If you want to free yourself from the weight of past pain, you need to confront it directly, to work through it rather than hide from it. Here are some strategies to help you face pain head-on, to process it in a way that brings true release, and to move forward lighter, stronger, and unburdened.

## Strategy #1: Create a Safe Space for Pain

Facing pain requires a sense of safety. You need a space where you can be fully vulnerable, a place where you don't have to hold back or pretend. This space can be physical—like a private room, a cozy spot in your home, or somewhere in nature where you feel at peace. Or it can be mental—a journal, a trusted friend, a therapist, or even a meditation practice.

In this space, allow yourself to feel what you're feeling without judgment. Give yourself permission to cry, to scream, to write out every raw thought you've been holding back. Creating a safe space for pain isn't about finding answers right away; it's about letting the pain surface so it can be acknowledged. By setting aside time to sit with your feelings, you're making a conscious choice to face the pain rather than run from it.

## Strategy #2: Lean on Your Breath

When pain feels overwhelming, your body reacts—your breath gets shallow, your muscles tense, your mind races. One of the most grounding tools you have in these moments is your breath. Breathing deeply and intentionally can help you reconnect with yourself, slow down the intensity, and make it easier to sit with the discomfort.

Try this: inhale deeply through your nose for a count of four, hold for four, then exhale slowly through your mouth for a count of six. Repeat this for a few minutes, focusing on the feeling of your breath moving in and out. This technique calms your nervous system, bringing your mind and body back into alignment, so you can approach your pain from a place of calm rather than panic.

## Strategy #3: Break It Down

Pain can feel massive, like an unscalable wall that you'll never get over. But often, what feels overwhelming is actually a collection of smaller, specific hurts. Take some time to break down your pain into individual parts. Write out the different aspects that are causing you distress—maybe it's betrayal, regret, loss, disappointment, or anger.

Once you've identified these parts, you can start addressing them one by one. Breaking down your pain makes it more manageable. You're no longer facing a vague, insurmountable feeling; you're dealing with specific issues that you can start to process, understand, and work through. It's a way of making the pain feel less overwhelming, of giving yourself a path forward.

## Strategy #4: Find the Words

Sometimes, pain is hard to process because it doesn't have words. It's just a feeling—a weight in your chest, a tightness in your stomach. But when you find a way to describe it, to put it into language, you start to make sense of it. Writing is one of the most powerful tools for this. Start by describing exactly what you're feeling. Be as detailed as you can—name the emotions, the sensations, the memories that come up.

If writing isn't your thing, you might try speaking your feelings aloud, either to yourself or to someone you trust. When you find the words, you're no longer at the mercy of your pain. You're able to name it, to understand it, to give it shape, and in doing so, you're taking back control.

## Strategy #5: Use Movement as Release

Pain isn't just mental; it's physical. It lives in your body, settling into your muscles, your posture, even the way you hold yourself. Movement can help release pain that's become stored in your body. Try activities that let you release tension and connect with yourself—yoga, running, dancing, or even just going for a long walk. Physical activity helps clear your mind, improves your mood, and allows your body to let go of the stress and tension that come with holding onto pain.

If you're dealing with intense emotions, consider movement that's expressive, like dancing to music that resonates with your mood or punching a pillow if you're feeling angry. Movement releases pent-up energy, giving your body a way to process emotions in a way that words sometimes can't.

## Strategy #6: Embrace Self-Compassion

Pain often brings self-criticism. Maybe you blame yourself for what happened, or you feel weak for struggling to move on. But the truth is, pain is universal, and it's okay to struggle.

Embracing self-compassion is about treating yourself with the same kindness you would offer a friend. It's about saying, "This hurts, and that's okay. I'm doing the best I can."

Practice speaking to yourself in a gentle, encouraging way. Remind yourself that it's okay to feel, that you're allowed to take your time to heal. Self-compassion isn't about pitying yourself; it's about recognizing that pain is hard, and you're worthy of patience and understanding as you work through it. When you give yourself compassion, you make room for healing to begin.

## Strategy #7: Seek Support Without Shame

Finally, know that you don't have to face pain alone. Sometimes, working through pain requires support from others—whether that's friends, family, a therapist, or a support group. There's no shame in asking for help. In fact, reaching out for support is one of the bravest things you can do.

Talk to people who make you feel safe, who can offer a listening ear without judgment. Share what you're going through, or even just sit in their presence if you're not ready to talk. Support gives you perspective, reminding you that you're not alone in your struggle. It's a way of lightening the load, of letting others share in the weight so that it's not so overwhelming.

---

These strategies aren't quick fixes—they're tools to help you approach your pain with intention and courage. Working through pain is a process, one that requires patience, honesty, and resilience. But each time you choose to face it rather than avoid it, you're building a path toward freedom. You're moving closer to a place where pain no longer controls you, where it's part of your experience but not the whole of it. Embracing your pain, processing it fully, is the path to healing and, ultimately, to finding a sense of peace.

Letting go of pain doesn't mean forgetting what happened. It's not about erasing memories or pretending you weren't affected by them. Letting go is about releasing the hold that pain has over your present and future. It's about freeing yourself from reliving the hurt over and over, from carrying it like a weight that stops you from moving forward. Letting go isn't about dismissing your experiences; it's about reclaiming your life from the grip of the past.

The first step in letting go is acceptance. This is one of the hardest parts because it means coming to terms with the fact that what's done is done. You can't change what happened, and you can't rewrite the past. Acceptance doesn't mean you agree with or condone what happened. It just means you're choosing to stop fighting against reality. When you accept what happened, you're no longer expending energy on "what ifs" or "if onlys." You're allowing yourself to come to terms with the past so that you can start focusing on the present.

Another key to letting go is shifting your focus. Pain has a way of keeping your mind stuck in a loop, replaying events, dwelling on details, and amplifying your suffering. To let go, you have to begin redirecting your focus. This doesn't mean avoiding your feelings; it means choosing where to place your attention. Practice noticing when your mind drifts back to painful memories and gently guide yourself back to the present. Focus on things you're grateful for, activities that bring you peace, or goals that give you a sense of purpose. The more you practice this, the more your brain learns to prioritize the present over the past.

One of the most liberating ways to let go is through forgiveness—not necessarily for others, but for yourself. You might be carrying feelings of guilt, shame, or regret over things you think you could have done differently. Forgive yourself for being human, for making decisions with the knowledge you had at the time. Self-forgiveness is about acknowledging that you're not perfect, and that's okay. It's about accepting that you did the best you could with what you knew, and now, you're choosing to move forward with compassion instead of criticism.

Letting go also means releasing the need for closure. Sometimes, the answers we want or the apologies we're waiting for never come. People may not acknowledge their role in our pain, and situations may never be fully resolved. Part of letting go is accepting that closure is something you create for yourself, not something you wait for others to give you. You can decide that you're done waiting, that you're moving on with or without an apology, with or without an explanation. Closure is a choice, a decision to stop looking back and start looking forward, even when things remain unresolved.

If you find yourself struggling to let go, try visualizing the process. Imagine your pain as a physical weight, something you've been carrying for a long time. Picture yourself slowly putting it down, piece by piece, allowing it to sink into the ground. Feel the weight lifting from your shoulders, your chest, your heart. Visualization can be a powerful way to reinforce your intention to release what no longer serves you. It's a reminder that you have the power to put down what you've been carrying and walk away lighter, freer.

Letting go doesn't erase the past, but it transforms your relationship to it. It allows you to remember without being held captive by the memories. It enables you to honor your experiences without letting them define you. You're not forgetting what happened; you're acknowledging that it happened, that it impacted you, and that now, you're choosing to live in a way that's no longer weighed down by it.

The power in letting go lies in reclaiming your energy, your focus, and your sense of self. It's about making a conscious choice to invest in your present and future rather than being tethered to a painful past. When you let go, you're not saying the pain didn't matter. You're saying it doesn't have to control your life anymore. You're choosing freedom, strength, and peace. And that choice is the ultimate act of healing.

# Chapter 8: Reclaim Your Power

Taking back your power starts with identifying where, and to whom, you gave it away. Power isn't always about control or authority; it's about your right to make choices that align with who you are, to stand by your boundaries, and to live in a way that honors your values. Over time, through relationships, experiences, or societal conditioning, it's easy to let parts of yourself slip away. Maybe you started compromising to keep the peace, stopped speaking up to avoid conflict, or let others' expectations dictate your decisions. Slowly, piece by piece, you handed over parts of yourself until one day, you woke up feeling disconnected, wondering where your sense of self went.

The first step to reclaiming your power is to recognize these moments, to get honest about the places where you've let others have influence over your choices, your thoughts, and your beliefs. Think back to times when you've ignored your intuition, when you've stayed silent, or when you've let someone else's opinion outweigh your own. Maybe it was in a relationship where you kept quiet to avoid confrontation, or in a job where you suppressed your creativity to meet someone else's standards. Each of these moments, small as they might seem, is an example of where your power leaked out—where you made the choice to prioritize others over yourself.

Reclaiming your power isn't about looking back with regret; it's about identifying these moments and understanding that you have the choice to act differently moving forward. It's about saying, "This is where I gave away my voice, my peace, my confidence, but now, I'm taking it back." Self-awareness is the foundation here because until you recognize where you've compromised yourself, it's difficult to make meaningful changes.

Next, you need to start setting boundaries with intention. Boundaries are the backbone of personal power. They're the lines you draw to protect your time, your energy, and your emotional well-being. Take a moment to ask yourself: *Where do I feel drained? Where do I feel like I'm always giving, without getting anything in return?* These areas are often where you're giving too much of yourself away. Setting boundaries doesn't mean shutting people out; it means deciding how much access they have to you. It's about respecting yourself enough to say, "This is what I need to feel whole, to feel balanced, to feel true to myself."

Another critical step is learning to trust your intuition. Over time, the noise of others' opinions and expectations can drown out your inner voice. You might find yourself second-guessing decisions, hesitating when it comes to standing by what feels right. Reclaiming your power means reconnecting with that inner guidance, trusting yourself again. Start by paying attention to what your gut is telling you, to the subtle nudges that steer you toward certain choices and away from others. Intuition is a powerful guide, but it requires trust and practice. The more you listen to it, the stronger it becomes, and the more confident you'll feel in following it.

One of the most empowering ways to reclaim your power is by redefining your self-worth. When you rely on external validation—whether that's approval from family, acceptance from friends, or praise at work—you're giving away power over your own sense of worth. Reclaiming your power means shifting that source of validation inward. It's about finding worth in who you are, not in what others think of you. Remind yourself of your values, your strengths, and your unique qualities. Build a foundation of self-worth that doesn't need constant reinforcement from outside sources. When you validate yourself, you're no longer at the mercy of others' opinions; you're standing firm in a self-worth that can't be taken away.

Lastly, reclaiming your power requires courage—the courage to say no, to walk away from situations that no longer serve you, to be unapologetically yourself. Reclaiming your power is a declaration that you deserve to take up space, to live by your own rules, to honor your needs without feeling guilty. It's a commitment to making decisions that align with who you are, even when they're difficult. Because at the end of the day, power isn't about controlling anyone else; it's about choosing to be fully, authentically in control of your own life.

Boundaries are essential to reclaiming your power, yet they're often misunderstood. Many people think of boundaries as walls, barriers that keep others at a distance. But real boundaries aren't about shutting people out; they're about creating a framework for healthy relationships, a guide for how you interact with others in a way that respects both your needs and theirs. Boundaries are the lines that protect your peace, your time, and your energy. They're the way you communicate, "This is what I need to feel whole, and this is what I'm willing to give." When you set boundaries, you're reclaiming control over your life, and you're doing it in a way that fosters connection rather than isolation.

The first step in setting boundaries is identifying where you feel consistently drained, resentful, or uncomfortable. Think of boundaries as a form of emotional self-defense—if there are areas in your life that leave you feeling exhausted, overwhelmed, or undervalued, it's likely because boundaries are lacking there. Start with one or two areas where you feel the need for boundaries the most, whether that's with family, friends, work, or even your own inner critic. Boundaries can be as much about protecting your inner peace as they are about interacting with others.

When you're ready to set a boundary, keep it clear and straightforward. Boundaries don't have to be complicated or harsh; they just need to communicate your needs in a direct way. For example, if you need time for yourself, say something like, "I need some alone time on weekends to recharge." Or if a friend constantly brings up topics that stress you out, try saying, "I'd rather not discuss this topic right now—it's something I'm working on processing." Boundaries are most effective when they're clear, respectful, and consistent.

The real challenge of setting boundaries isn't in stating them—it's in enforcing them. Often, when we set boundaries, we worry about how others will react. We fear they'll be hurt, disappointed, or even angry. But here's the thing: when you set boundaries, it's not your job to manage others' emotions; it's your job to protect your well-being. You can be kind and empathetic, but you don't have to sacrifice your peace to keep others comfortable. Remember, boundaries are about self-respect, not people-pleasing. You're teaching others how to treat you by showing them what you will and won't accept.

Another key to effective boundaries is consistency. If you set a boundary but then constantly let it slide, people will learn that it doesn't really matter. Consistency reinforces that your boundaries are important to you, and over time, people will begin to respect them without pushing back. For instance, if you've set a boundary around work emails after hours, don't respond to them outside of that time. If you've established a personal boundary around negative topics with friends, gently remind them each time the subject comes up. Consistency is what turns boundaries from ideas into realities, and it helps you build a life that honors your limits.

Boundaries can also be flexible—they don't have to be rigid or absolute. Sometimes, the healthiest boundaries are the ones that can adapt to specific situations while still respecting your core needs. For example, maybe your boundary around alone time shifts during holidays, or your boundary around work changes during a big project. Flexibility doesn't mean abandoning your boundaries; it means recognizing when they can adapt without compromising your peace. It's about knowing that you can bend without breaking, adjust without losing your center.

One important thing to remember is that boundaries will sometimes push people away—and that's okay. Not everyone will understand or respect your boundaries, and some may even try to challenge them. But those who genuinely care for you will respect your need for space, for self-care, for honesty. They'll understand that boundaries aren't about rejecting them; they're about honoring both of you. Boundaries allow for healthier, more authentic connections because they create space for both parties to show up as they are, without resentment or exhaustion clouding the relationship.

Ultimately, boundaries are a form of self-love. They're a way of saying, "I deserve to protect my time, my energy, and my mental well-being." They allow you to show up as the best version of yourself, fully present and unburdened. Boundaries don't limit relationships—they enhance them, because when you're clear about what you need, you can give from a place of fullness rather than depletion. So start small, be consistent, and remember: setting boundaries is one of the most powerful ways to reclaim your peace and your power.

One of the most liberating ways to reclaim your power is to let go of the need for validation. From a young age, most of us are conditioned to seek approval—to be liked, praised, and accepted. We're taught that other people's opinions of us hold value, that we're "good" or "worthy" when we meet the standards others set. But relying on validation from others keeps you trapped in a cycle where your self-worth is dependent on their acceptance. It hands over control of your life, leaving you constantly questioning, adjusting, and compromising just to feel "enough." Reclaiming your power means learning to trust your own voice, to find validation within, rather than depending on others to affirm who you are.

The first step to releasing the need for validation is to recognize when and why you seek it. Notice those moments when you feel the need to check in with others, when you feel a pull to share achievements, or when you're hesitant to make a decision until someone else has approved it. Ask yourself, *Why do I need their validation? Am I afraid of making a mistake? Am I worried about how I'll be perceived?* Often, the need for validation is rooted in fear—fear of rejection, fear of failure, or fear of judgment. But these fears don't define you. They're simply reminders that you're human, that you're wired to seek connection. Understanding this can help you let go of the need for validation with compassion, not judgment.

One of the most effective ways to build self-trust is to start validating yourself, one small step at a time. Begin by affirming your decisions, even the small ones, without seeking input from others. Trust yourself to make choices that align with your values, even if they're unconventional or go against the grain. Each time you make a decision on your own, you're reinforcing that you're capable, that your opinion is valid, that you don't need anyone else's stamp of approval to know what's right for you. The more you practice self-validation, the easier it becomes to rely on your own voice rather than looking to others for answers.

Another powerful tool for reclaiming your power is self-reflection. After a significant decision, take a moment to reflect on how it felt. Did the choice align with your values? Did it bring you closer to the life you want? Reflecting in this way allows you to see that you're capable of making good decisions without outside input. It builds confidence and shows you that your intuition, your preferences, and your values are trustworthy guides. Over time, self-reflection becomes a way of reinforcing self-validation, a way of showing yourself that your decisions are enough, no matter what others might think.

Releasing the need for validation also requires self-compassion. There will be times when you question yourself, when you feel insecure, when you're tempted to seek approval just to ease the uncertainty. In these moments, remind yourself that it's okay to feel unsure. Self-compassion is about accepting yourself fully, even in moments of doubt. It's about speaking kindly to yourself, forgiving your mistakes, and allowing yourself to grow. When you're compassionate toward yourself, you create a space where self-trust can flourish, where your voice can grow louder and clearer.

One effective exercise for building self-validation is creating a "strengths journal." Every day, write down one thing you did that made you proud or one quality you appreciate in yourself. Over time, you'll build a record of your strengths, your decisions, and your values. This journal becomes a tangible reminder of everything you're capable of, a resource you can look back on whenever you start doubting yourself. It reinforces that your self-worth doesn't come from outside approval but from within, from knowing who you are and what you stand for.

Letting go of the need for validation isn't about isolating yourself or rejecting others' support; it's about finding a stable foundation within so that others' opinions don't define your worth. It's about knowing that your value doesn't rise and fall based on external feedback. Reclaiming your power is about trusting that you know yourself best and that your choices, guided by your intuition and values, are enough. When you let go of the need for validation, you're no longer swayed by the tides of others' opinions. You're rooted, grounded, and empowered to live authentically, to make choices that feel right for you, regardless of what anyone else thinks.

True self-worth isn't something that fluctuates based on how others see you or how well you meet their expectations. It's an internal compass, a sense of value that comes from within and doesn't depend on anyone else's opinion. When you cultivate unshakeable self-worth, you're no longer at the mercy of external validation, achievements, or the roles you play. You're rooted in a belief that you're enough, exactly as you are. Building this foundation takes time, but it's one of the most powerful ways to reclaim your power and live a life that's true to you.

The first step in building unshakeable self-worth is recognizing that you are more than your accomplishments, your appearance, or your social status. You are inherently valuable simply because you exist. Society often ties self-worth to success, appearance, or productivity, but these are external factors—they don't define the core of who you are. Remind yourself that your worth is innate. You don't have to earn it or prove it to anyone. Begin to separate your identity from the roles you play and the things you achieve. You are worthy, no matter what.

One powerful exercise to build self-worth is to identify and challenge negative self-talk. Often, we have an inner critic that constantly tells us we're not enough. This voice might say things like, "I'm not smart enough," or "I'll never succeed." These thoughts are not facts; they're limiting beliefs that weaken your sense of self. Each time you notice negative self-talk, challenge it. Ask yourself, "Is this really true? Is there evidence that disproves this thought?" Replace these criticisms with affirmations that reinforce your inherent worth, such as, "I am enough as I am," or "My value isn't defined by what I accomplish."

Another powerful strategy is to focus on your values rather than outcomes. Instead of tying your self-worth to achievements, tie it to the qualities and values you bring to the table. Are you compassionate, honest, resilient, or creative? These are traits that no one can take away from you, traits that define who you are regardless of any external circumstances. When you live in alignment with your values, you're building a life that reflects your true self, not just your accomplishments. Each time you act according to your values, you reinforce your worth in a way that's independent of others' approval or success metrics.

Self-worth also grows when you practice self-care. This isn't just about bubble baths or relaxing activities; it's about honoring your needs, setting boundaries, and investing in your well-being. Self-care is a statement of self-respect. It's a way of saying, "I matter enough to take care of myself." Make a habit of prioritizing your mental, emotional, and physical health. When you take care of yourself, you're sending a message that you're worthy of care, compassion, and kindness. Self-care is a tangible way of affirming your value, of treating yourself with the respect you deserve.

Building self-worth also involves surrounding yourself with people who respect you. Healthy relationships reflect back your worth rather than diminish it. Choose to spend time with people who support your growth, who encourage you to be yourself, and who value you for who you are, not for what you can do for them. These relationships become a mirror, reflecting the worth you're cultivating within. Toxic relationships, on the other hand, can erode self-worth, so be mindful of who you allow into your inner circle. Choose people who respect your boundaries, who bring positivity into your life, and who remind you of your inherent value.

Lastly, self-worth becomes unshakeable when you give yourself permission to be imperfect. Perfectionism is a thief of self-worth. It convinces you that you're only valuable if you're flawless, if you make no mistakes. But perfection is an illusion. Real self-worth means embracing all parts of yourself, including the messy, imperfect parts. Give yourself permission to fail, to make mistakes, and to grow through them. Remember, you're worthy of love and respect even when you fall short. Self-worth is about knowing that you're enough, flaws and all.

Building self-worth that can't be shaken is about treating yourself with the kindness, respect, and compassion you deserve. It's about learning to be your own greatest supporter, to stand by yourself regardless of external circumstances. This foundation of self-worth empowers you to live authentically, to take risks, and to make choices that align with who you are. When your self-worth is rooted within, no one else has the power to take it away. You are enough—exactly as you are—and the more you believe that, the more powerful, resilient, and free you become.

Chapter 9

# Chapter 9: Live Unapologetically

Living unapologetically means showing up exactly as you are, without feeling the need to explain, justify, or filter yourself to fit into someone else's version of "acceptable." It's about giving yourself permission to take up space, to own your quirks, your opinions, your boundaries, and to let go of the constant worry about how others might perceive you. When you live unapologetically, you're free to be your true self, flaws and all, because you're no longer dependent on anyone else's validation.

One of the biggest barriers to living unapologetically is the belief that you have to be "good enough" by someone else's standards. Maybe you've been taught to keep your voice down, to smooth over your rough edges, to adjust your personality so that you're likable, agreeable, or easy to get along with. But all of these expectations are limiting. They keep you from experiencing the full range of who you are and what you're capable of. Embracing your true self means realizing that you don't need to be "acceptable" to anyone other than yourself. Your worth isn't dependent on fitting into someone else's box.

Living unapologetically starts with self-acceptance. This means accepting all parts of yourself, including the parts you might consider messy or imperfect. It's acknowledging that you're not here to be flawless; you're here to be real. Self-acceptance doesn't mean ignoring your flaws or mistakes, but it does mean refusing to be ashamed of them. When you accept yourself fully, you take away the power that shame or self-criticism holds over you. You're no longer hiding parts of yourself or feeling like you have to apologize for who you are.

Start by identifying the parts of yourself that you've been hiding or downplaying. Maybe it's a passion you've been keeping quiet about, an opinion you don't usually voice, or a part of your personality that feels "too much." Ask yourself: *Why am I hiding this part of myself? Am I afraid of judgment? Am I worried about being misunderstood?* Once you understand the reasons behind these feelings, you can start challenging them. Remind yourself that you're not here to meet everyone's expectations, that the only person you need to answer to is yourself.

Living unapologetically also means letting go of the need to explain your choices. When you make a decision that aligns with your values or boundaries, you don't owe anyone a justification. You don't have to explain why you chose to walk away from a relationship, why you turned down a certain opportunity, or why you live your life the way you do. The need to explain yourself often comes from a place of wanting approval, of hoping that if others understand, they'll accept you. But the truth is, your choices are valid, even if no one else understands them. Your life is yours to live, not something that needs to be approved or validated by others.

One exercise to start living unapologetically is to create a personal manifesto. Write down a declaration of who you are, what you stand for, and what you refuse to apologize for. This manifesto might include statements like, "I am allowed to take up space," "I am proud of my strengths and my flaws," or "I live by my own standards, not anyone else's." This document is your permission slip to be unapologetically you. Keep it somewhere visible, and read it whenever you feel the pull to shrink yourself, to blend in, or to apologize for who you are.

Living unapologetically is an act of courage. It's choosing to be your true self in a world that often pressures you to conform. It's standing by yourself, even when others don't get it, even when people question you, and even when it feels uncomfortable. But in that courage, you find freedom. You find the power to live authentically, to make choices that reflect your values, and to build a life that resonates with who you truly are.

Here's the bottom line: you don't need to be "acceptable." You just need to be real. You need to be true to yourself, even if it means standing out, even if it means disappointing others who expected you to fit their mold. Because living unapologetically isn't about fitting in—it's about breaking free from the need to fit in. It's about owning every part of yourself and giving yourself permission to exist without apology. And that's the ultimate form of self-respect.

When you choose to live unapologetically, you're going to disappoint people. It's inevitable. People have expectations—whether they're your friends, family, coworkers, or society at large. They might expect you to behave a certain way, to agree with their opinions, to make decisions that align with what they believe is best. But living for others' expectations is a recipe for constant compromise. You end up prioritizing their comfort over your truth, and that's a trade-off that only leads to resentment and burnout.

Making peace with disappointing others is about recognizing that you can't please everyone, and that's okay. In fact, it's healthy. Living authentically means sometimes choosing what's right for you, even if it makes others uncomfortable. You're allowed to set boundaries, to say no, to take a different path. Disappointment is not a reflection of your worth; it's a reflection of others' expectations, which aren't your responsibility to fulfill.

The first step in making peace with disappointing others is acknowledging that their reactions don't define you. You're not responsible for managing how others feel about your choices. Their disappointment doesn't mean you're wrong, selfish, or unkind. It simply means you made a decision that prioritized your needs or values over theirs. This doesn't make you a bad person; it makes you someone who respects themselves enough to choose authenticity over conformity.

It's helpful to remind yourself that disappointment is a temporary reaction. People adapt, even if they don't agree with or understand your choices initially. In most cases, those who genuinely care about you will come to respect your decisions, even if it takes time. And if they don't? That's a reflection of their inability to accept you for who you are, not a reason for you to change. Remember, relationships based on authenticity are far more fulfilling than those built on constant compromise and appeasement.

Another important part of handling others' disappointment is learning to sit with your own discomfort. There may be times when you feel guilty for putting your needs first, especially if you're used to prioritizing others. But guilt doesn't mean you're wrong—it's simply a reaction to breaking patterns you've been conditioned to follow. Challenge that guilt by asking yourself, *Am I making this choice because it aligns with who I am, or am I choosing it to avoid disappointing someone else?* The more you prioritize choices that reflect your truth, the less power guilt will have over you.

One exercise to help you embrace disappointing others without guilt is to create a "Self-Respect List." Write down the qualities, values, and boundaries that matter most to you. This list serves as a reminder of what you're committed to, even if others don't agree. When you make a choice that's true to these values and someone else feels disappointed, return to this list. It's a way of reaffirming that your decisions are grounded in what genuinely matters to you, rather than in the need to please.

Living unapologetically doesn't mean you don't care about others' feelings; it means you care about your own feelings enough to let them guide you. It's about recognizing that your well-being, your growth, and your peace are valid priorities. You're not here to fulfill someone else's version of who you should be. You're here to live in alignment with who you truly are. Disappointment from others is just a byproduct of choosing authenticity over approval.

Ultimately, staying true to yourself means honoring your journey, even when others don't understand it. The right people will respect you for it, and those who don't were never meant to walk that path with you. Making peace with disappointing others isn't about dismissing their feelings—it's about giving yourself permission to live a life that's true to you, a life where your self-respect matters more than external approval. When you embrace that freedom, you'll find that your relationships become more honest, your decisions feel more aligned, and your life becomes a reflection of your true self, unburdened by the weight of others' expectations.

Expressing yourself authentically is one of the most freeing things you can do, but it's not always easy. Sometimes, being real means risking rejection, facing judgment, or stepping outside your comfort zone. Authentic self-expression isn't just about speaking your truth when it's convenient; it's about showing up as yourself, especially when it's hard. Living unapologetically means learning to express your thoughts, your needs, and your feelings openly, without censoring yourself to fit others' expectations.

One of the biggest challenges to authentic expression is the fear of vulnerability. When you express your true self, you're showing others who you really are—your strengths, your values, your passions, but also your doubts, your fears, and your insecurities. Vulnerability can be uncomfortable because it's raw and unfiltered, but it's also what makes you relatable and human. It's what connects you to others on a deeper level. When you let yourself be vulnerable, you're showing that you're real, and that kind of openness invites others to be real with you too.

To express yourself authentically, start by acknowledging your truth, even if it feels uncomfortable. Practice saying, "This is how I feel," or "This is what I need," without downplaying or sugarcoating it. You don't have to shout your truth from the rooftops, but you do need to own it. For example, if you feel strongly about a topic, share your opinion confidently, even if it's different from those around you. If you have a need in a relationship, express it directly rather than hoping the other person will just know. Owning your truth, in a calm and grounded way, reinforces that your voice deserves to be heard.

One of the most powerful tools for authentic expression is self-affirmation. Before a difficult conversation or a situation where you know you'll need to stand by your beliefs, take a moment to affirm your right to speak your truth. Tell yourself, "I deserve to be heard," or "My thoughts and feelings are valid." This self-affirmation helps build confidence, reminding you that your voice has value. It's a way of grounding yourself in your worth so that, no matter how others react, you know that your expression was a reflection of your true self.

A practical exercise to build authentic expression is the "Journal of Unfiltered Truth." Set aside time each day to write down your thoughts, emotions, and desires as honestly as possible, without worrying about how they sound or how someone else might react. This practice helps you get comfortable with your own voice. When you see your thoughts on paper, unfiltered and uncensored, you start to realize that they're valid, that they don't need to be adjusted for others. Over time, this comfort with your inner voice translates to more confidence in expressing it outwardly.

It's also helpful to embrace discomfort as part of the process. Authentic expression won't always feel easy or smooth, and that's okay. Sometimes, your voice may shake, or you might feel anxious afterward. But each time you choose to express yourself honestly, you're building resilience. You're proving to yourself that you can face the discomfort and come out stronger. In time, the discomfort fades, and you'll find that expressing your truth becomes second nature, something that feels empowering rather than intimidating.

Remember, expressing yourself authentically isn't about forcing your opinions on others or expecting everyone to agree with you. It's about sharing who you are without feeling the need to edit, explain, or shrink yourself to fit in. It's about being honest with yourself and with others, creating relationships and spaces where the real you can thrive. Authentic expression allows you to build connections based on mutual respect and understanding, rather than on pretense.

Living unapologetically means embracing every part of who you are, from your strengths to your insecurities, from your passions to your quirks. It's about letting your true self be seen, even when it's uncomfortable, because you know that being real is worth it. When you express yourself authentically, you're honoring your voice, your values, and your journey. You're showing up for yourself in a way that no one else can, and that's the ultimate form of self-respect.

Living unapologetically is rooted in self-respect. It's about holding yourself with dignity, standing by your values, and making choices that align with who you are. When self-respect becomes the foundation of your life, you're no longer willing to compromise yourself for approval or shrink yourself to avoid conflict. Self-respect means honoring your worth without conditions, accepting yourself without exceptions, and knowing that you deserve to live a life that reflects your truth.

Cultivating self-respect starts with setting standards for how you treat yourself. Too often, we tolerate behaviors, thoughts, or habits that diminish our sense of worth. Think about how you talk to yourself, how you treat your body, how you handle setbacks. Are you kind to yourself, or do you judge yourself harshly? Do you prioritize your well-being, or do you sacrifice it to meet others' needs? Self-respect means treating yourself as someone deserving of care, love, and patience. It means setting standards for how you talk to yourself, how you take care of yourself, and how you allow others to treat you.

One powerful practice for building self-respect is creating a list of "Non-Negotiables." These are the values, boundaries, and standards that you refuse to compromise on. For example:

- **"I will not tolerate disrespect from myself or others."**
- **"I will prioritize my mental and physical health."**
- **"I will make decisions that align with my values, even if it means standing alone."**
- **"I will be kind to myself, even in moments of failure."**

Non-negotiables act as a guide, reminding you of your worth every day. When you have clear standards for how you'll be treated, it becomes easier to make choices that honor yourself. You're no longer swayed by others' opinions or the pressure to conform, because you know what you stand for and what you won't accept.

Another key to self-respect is letting go of perfectionism. Perfectionism is the belief that you're only worthy if you're flawless, if you never make mistakes, if you meet every expectation. But self-respect isn't about being perfect; it's about being real. It's about accepting yourself fully, imperfections and all. When you respect yourself, you understand that you're worthy of love and respect, even when you fall short. You give yourself permission to grow, to learn from mistakes, to be a work in progress.

True self-respect means embracing your humanity, understanding that you're worthy because of who you are, not in spite of it.

Self-respect also involves honoring your intuition. That inner voice, the one that knows what's right for you, is one of your most powerful guides. When you respect yourself, you trust that intuition, even when it leads you in a direction others might not understand. Following your intuition reinforces that your voice, your feelings, and your perspective matter. You're choosing to live by your own standards, to follow what feels true to you, rather than constantly looking for validation outside of yourself.

Another practical way to cultivate self-respect is to practice saying "no" without apology. Self-respect means knowing your limits and being willing to protect your time, energy, and peace. When you respect yourself, you're not afraid to say no to things that drain you, to relationships that don't honor you, or to obligations that don't align with your values. Saying no doesn't make you selfish; it makes you self-respecting. It shows that you're willing to protect your well-being, even if it means disappointing others. Each time you say no to something that doesn't serve you, you're saying yes to a life that aligns with who you are.

Finally, self-respect grows when you celebrate your wins, no matter how small. Acknowledging your achievements, giving yourself credit, and taking pride in your progress reinforce the message that you're worthy of recognition. When you respect yourself, you don't wait for others to validate you; you become your own source of validation. Take a moment each day to appreciate something you did well, to recognize your growth, to thank yourself for showing up. This small habit of self-acknowledgment builds a sense of self-worth that no one else can give you.

Living unapologetically, at its core, is about respecting yourself enough to be real. It's about honoring your truth, standing by your values, and giving yourself permission to take up space. Self-respect is the foundation that supports all of this. When you respect yourself, you don't feel the need to apologize for who you are or the life you choose to live. You're free to be fully, unapologetically you, and that's a freedom that transforms everything.

# Chapter 10: The Strength in Vulnerability

In my first book, I wrote about survival. About the grit it takes to keep going when life has chewed you up and spit you out. But here's the thing I didn't fully understand until later: survival is only part of the story. To truly live, you have to let down the guard that survival forced you to build. And that's where vulnerability comes in—not as a weakness, but as the raw, real strength it takes to step into your own story without armor, without apology. Vulnerability isn't about being "soft" or "emotional" or whatever labels the world throws at it; it's about having the guts to be open, to be honest, and to show up fully, even if it means getting hurt.

If you grew up anything like I did, vulnerability was a luxury. When your focus is just making it through the day, who has time for all that "feeling" stuff? For years, I thought vulnerability was just something to keep tucked away, something only people with safe, easy lives could afford. But I was wrong. Vulnerability is what lets us access our own humanity, connect with others, and—most of all—heal. It's what turns pain into purpose, what turns survival into strength. And if we don't let ourselves be vulnerable, then we're just walking around with our fists up, waiting for the next blow.

Let me say it straight: vulnerability is terrifying. Opening up feels like you're just waiting for someone to take advantage of that openness, to poke at that wound. But here's what I learned—the more you run from vulnerability, the more you're running from yourself. It keeps you stuck in survival mode, trapped in that constant fight-or-flight mindset, never fully able to relax, trust, or love. Vulnerability is strength because it allows you to show up, to take off the armor, and to say, "This is me." It's saying, "I've been through hell, but I'm still here, and I'm not hiding anymore."

In this chapter, I want to break down what it means to embrace vulnerability as a tool, a superpower, not a liability. Vulnerability isn't something we're taught to respect or value, but it's the very thing that lets us create a life we're not just surviving in but thriving in. So many people, myself included, go through life guarding every part of themselves, holding onto the pain, the anger, the regret, as if hiding those things makes them less real. But it's only when we stop hiding, when we let others see us—scars, rage, mistakes, and all—that we start to heal. And more than that, we start to feel alive.

The strength in vulnerability isn't in the act of baring your soul for anyone who'll listen. It's in choosing when and how to let yourself be seen. It's knowing that you're still in control, but this time, instead of using control to protect yourself, you're using it to empower yourself. You're saying, "I'm strong enough to be real." It's not about oversharing or spilling your guts for sympathy. It's about letting the people who matter see the parts of you that you've hidden for too long. It's about standing tall in your truth, not because it's easy, but because you're worth that kind of honesty.

And let me tell you—when you start living with that level of openness, things shift. People will either come closer, drawn to that realness, or they'll back away, unable to handle it. And that's okay. Vulnerability has a way of cutting through the noise, of showing you who's meant to walk this path with you and who isn't. The ones who can handle your truth, who respect your scars and honor your story, are the ones who deserve to be there. And the ones who can't? They were never going to love the real you anyway. Vulnerability acts like a filter; it clears out the people who don't belong and leaves space for those who do.

Choosing vulnerability is choosing to live fully. It's about giving yourself permission to feel, to connect, to risk being hurt because you know that the alternative is just staying numb, staying safe, but never really living. Vulnerability is standing in the mirror and saying, "I accept every part of me—even the parts that hurt." It's what allows us to break down the walls we built to survive, to let people in, and to finally live a life that's honest, messy, and completely, unapologetically ours.

So here's my truth, the one I had to learn the hard way: Vulnerability isn't a curse. It's a gift. And the moment you choose to see it that way, to embrace it instead of running from it, you're no longer just surviving—you're stepping into the power of truly living.

The people who matter in your life are the ones who can handle your truth—the ones who don't need you to put on a show or pretend everything is fine. When you allow yourself to be vulnerable, you're creating a doorway to real connection. You're saying, "This is who I am, no filter, no edits." And when people see that and still choose to stand by you, those are the connections that last. Those are the people who matter.

For years, I kept my guard up. I thought that if I let people see the real, unpolished version of myself, they'd run the other way. And sure, some people did. But the ones who stayed? They became my true circle, the people who saw my cracks and respected me all the more for them. Vulnerability became the test, the filter. It allowed me to cut through the small talk, the pretending, and get down to who was really there for me and who wasn't.

Vulnerability doesn't mean you're opening up to everyone, spilling your guts to every person you meet. It's not about oversharing or putting yourself on display. It's about discerning who deserves to see those parts of you and then having the courage to let them in. When you're vulnerable with someone, you're giving them access to a part of you that's real, that's raw. It's an invitation, not an expectation. And if they can't handle it? That's on them, not you. Vulnerability has a way of cutting out the people who can't handle depth, who are only around for the good times, and it leaves you with the people who are willing to stand in the mess with you.

Here's something I had to learn the hard way: not everyone deserves access to your vulnerability. You have the right to choose who sees the real you. Vulnerability is a gift, one you give to those who've shown they can be trusted with it. If you open up to someone and they dismiss you, judge you, or use it against you, that's a clear sign they don't belong in your inner circle. Real connection is built on mutual respect, understanding, and acceptance. If someone can't honor your vulnerability, they're not respecting who you truly are, and they don't deserve the privilege of your openness.

One of the most important things vulnerability does is allow others to feel safe being real with you. When you're open about your own struggles, your own fears, you give others permission to drop their guard too. It's like saying, "Hey, it's okay to be human here." You're creating a space where both of you can exist without the masks, without the pretending, and that's where true connection happens. People respond to realness. They feel it. When you're vulnerable, you're showing up as you are, and that invites others to do the same.

So, if you want connections that go deeper than surface level, start by being real with yourself. Stop filtering, stop editing, stop worrying about being "too much" or "not enough." If someone can't handle who you are, then they're not the kind of connection that's going to bring value to your life. Vulnerability weeds out the fake connections by stripping away the need for approval. It shows you who's willing to stick around when things aren't pretty, who's there because they see you, not just the version you present to the world.

When you embrace vulnerability, you'll start noticing a shift. People who are looking for shallow connections will drift away, but the ones who are drawn to depth will come closer. And yes, it's scary to open yourself up like that, to take the risk that someone might not understand, might not stay. But it's a risk worth taking, because what you gain in return is connection that's built on truth, not pretense.

Vulnerability is the foundation of any lasting relationship. It's the glue that holds people together through the good, the bad, and the downright ugly. It's what lets you be fully seen and still fully loved. And when you're surrounded by people who see and accept you for who you are, flaws and all, you're no longer living with that fear of being "found out." You're just you. And that's the kind of life worth living—a life where you're not hiding, not shrinking, but standing tall in your truth, surrounded by people who respect you enough to do the same.

Vulnerability will always be a risk, but it's also the reward. It's what turns strangers into family, what turns acquaintances into friends, what turns a life spent "getting by" into a life of real, lasting connections. And that's why it's worth every bit of discomfort, every bit of courage it takes to be real.

Embracing vulnerability isn't something that happens overnight. It's a practice, one that requires intention, patience, and courage. But with each small step, you start to feel the walls come down, and life becomes richer, more connected, more real. Here are some practical steps to start embracing vulnerability in your daily life—ways to show up as the real you, little by little, without needing to hide.

**Step 1: Start Small**

The first step to embracing vulnerability is to start small. You don't need to jump straight into sharing your deepest fears or painful memories with everyone around you. Begin with small acts of openness in your daily interactions. This might look like admitting when you don't know something, sharing a bit about your day that didn't go as planned, or expressing your opinion, even if it differs from others. These small moments of authenticity build a foundation, and over time, they make it easier to be open about bigger things.

For example, if a friend asks how you're doing, resist the urge to say, "I'm fine," if that's not the truth. Try something like, "It's been a tough week, but I'm getting through it." This kind of honesty invites connection without feeling like you're baring your entire soul all at once. Vulnerability can start as simply as being real in the moment.

## Step 2: Practice Self-Acceptance

Vulnerability requires self-acceptance because you can't be open with others if you're still hiding from yourself. Spend time acknowledging and accepting the parts of you that you've kept in the shadows—the fears, the insecurities, the mistakes. One effective way to do this is through journaling. Set aside a few minutes each day to write about what you're feeling without judgment. Get comfortable with your own emotions, even the uncomfortable ones.

When you start embracing these parts of yourself, they lose their power to control you. Self-acceptance isn't about loving every part of yourself unconditionally; it's about recognizing that every part of you, even the messy bits, are valid. This internal acceptance creates a safe space within you—a space where you can be real without shame. The more comfortable you are with your own flaws, the easier it becomes to share them with others.

## Step 3: Share Your Goals and Dreams

One simple way to practice vulnerability is to start sharing your dreams and goals with others. This might sound simple, but it's actually a powerful act of openness. Dreams are personal, and sharing them can make you feel exposed, as if you're giving people a glimpse of your deepest hopes. But when you share your goals with people who support you, you're allowing them to connect with the most hopeful parts of you.

For example, if you've always wanted to start a business, write a book, or travel somewhere meaningful, let people close to you in on those dreams. Even if they don't fully understand, sharing what matters to you helps you feel more connected and grounded in what you want from life. And when people know your goals, they're more likely to encourage you, to help you, and to keep you motivated.

## Step 4: Express Your Needs and Boundaries

Being vulnerable also means asking for what you need, even when it feels uncomfortable. This might mean telling a friend you need support, asking your partner for reassurance, or setting a boundary with someone who's been crossing lines. A big part of vulnerability is expressing your needs without feeling guilty for them.

Let's say a friend is venting to you about their problems, and it's emotionally draining you. Practicing vulnerability might look like saying, "I want to be here for you, but I need to take a break and recharge right now." It's not easy, but expressing your boundaries and needs allows you to build relationships that respect who you are and what you need to feel whole. Vulnerability isn't just about sharing emotions; it's about honoring your own limits.

## Step 5: Accept Help Without Shame

One of the biggest hurdles to vulnerability is the belief that you should handle everything on your own. But there's real strength in knowing when to ask for help. Letting someone support you, whether it's in the form of advice, a listening ear, or even a hand with something practical, is an act of vulnerability. It's acknowledging that you can't (and don't have to) do it all alone.

When someone offers help, practice saying yes. Whether it's a coworker offering to take on a task or a friend wanting to check in on you, accept their support. Vulnerability is about allowing yourself to be seen, even when it means letting others witness your struggles. This act of openness reinforces that you're human, that you need connection, and that you're not afraid to rely on others. Letting people help builds trust, and it's a powerful way of forming deeper bonds with those around you.

## Step 6: Be Honest About Your Mistakes

Another way to embrace vulnerability is to own your mistakes. There's nothing more human than making a misstep, and yet, so many of us try to hide it when we mess up. Acknowledging your mistakes, without excuses or blame, shows self-respect and honesty. It's saying, "I did this, and I'm responsible for it." When you own your mistakes, you're taking accountability, but you're also showing others that it's okay to be imperfect.

If you've hurt someone or let someone down, be upfront. Apologize, explain where you went wrong, and let them see that you're committed to doing better. This isn't just about them; it's about you. It's about letting go of the fear of judgment and showing that you respect yourself enough to be real, even when it's uncomfortable. Vulnerability in owning mistakes shows that you're strong enough to acknowledge your flaws, and that level of honesty deepens trust in any relationship.

## Step 7: Celebrate Your Wins—Big and Small

Vulnerability isn't just about sharing the hard stuff; it's also about letting people see your joy, your pride, your excitement. For some of us, it feels easier to share struggles than to celebrate achievements. We worry that people will see us as arrogant, or that they won't care. But celebrating your wins—big or small—is an important part of vulnerability. It's letting yourself be seen in your happiest moments and allowing others to celebrate with you.

So, when something good happens, share it with people who support you. It might be a promotion, a project you completed, or even a personal breakthrough. Let yourself be vulnerable enough to feel proud and to invite others to share in that pride. Celebrating your wins shows that you're not afraid to recognize your worth and that you value yourself enough to share your joy with the people who matter.

---

Each of these steps brings you closer to embracing vulnerability as a strength, not a weakness. Vulnerability doesn't mean spilling everything to everyone—it means choosing honesty, embracing your humanity, and allowing yourself to be seen without apology. When you let yourself live with this kind of openness, you're not only building deeper connections with others; you're building a more honest, resilient, and fulfilling relationship with yourself.

There's a freedom that comes with letting yourself be seen—a kind of peace that only vulnerability can bring. When you've spent years hiding parts of yourself, censoring your thoughts, or keeping your emotions buried, vulnerability can feel like a rebellion. It's an act of liberation, a decision to stop living for approval or acceptance. Vulnerability lets you shed the weight of pretending, of performing, and finally just breathe. And in that space, you discover a life that's honest, grounded, and deeply fulfilling.

When you allow yourself to be vulnerable, you're no longer living with that constant need to edit yourself, to adjust who you are to fit others' expectations. You stop asking, *Will they like me? Will they judge me?* Instead, you start living in alignment with your own values, not someone else's. This isn't just about feeling good; it's about finding purpose. Vulnerability lets you connect with the things that truly matter, the things that align with your core self. When you're honest about who you are, you can start building a life that reflects that honesty, a life that resonates with your own truth.

One of the most powerful parts of vulnerability is that it helps you make peace with your past. By embracing your own story, the mistakes, the traumas, the scars—you stop hiding from the things that have shaped you. You're able to say, "This is part of who I am, and I'm not ashamed of it." Vulnerability gives you the strength to hold your past with compassion, rather than burying it or letting it dictate your worth. It lets you look at where you've been, and instead of feeling weighed down by it, you find purpose in it. Your story, as messy as it might be, becomes a source of strength, a reminder that you've survived and that every experience has brought you closer to who you are.

Allowing yourself to be seen also brings a deep sense of peace. When you're no longer hiding parts of yourself, you can rest. There's no more anxiety about keeping up a front, no more pressure to be perfect, no more shame over your flaws. Vulnerability teaches you that it's okay to be imperfect, that it's okay to have needs, to make mistakes, to be a work in progress. You realize that your worth isn't defined by what you hide; it's defined by who you are, fully and unapologetically. This acceptance brings a sense of peace that's grounding, a kind of inner stillness that no amount of external validation can match.

In the act of being vulnerable, you start to find your purpose. You stop living for other people's expectations and start focusing on what truly resonates with you. Vulnerability allows you to align with what brings you joy, meaning, and fulfillment. It helps you discover what you genuinely care about, beyond what others think you should care about. It might mean pursuing a passion you've kept hidden, expressing creativity you've held back, or sharing a story that others need to hear. Vulnerability isn't just a personal journey; it's a way of contributing to the world by showing up as your truest self, adding something real and unique to those around you.

Another beautiful thing about vulnerability is that it creates a ripple effect. When you allow yourself to be seen, you give others permission to do the same. Your courage to be real, to show up without hiding, inspires those around you to embrace their own truths. Vulnerability creates connection, but it also creates change. It breaks down the walls that keep us isolated, the expectations that keep us small. It invites authenticity into every space you occupy, letting others feel safe to be their true selves. In this way, vulnerability doesn't just transform your life; it transforms the lives of those you connect with, building a network of openness and honesty that makes everyone stronger.

Living vulnerably isn't about oversharing or exposing every detail of your life to the world. It's about being true to yourself, about choosing to be real in a world that often rewards pretense. It's about making peace with your past, accepting your imperfections, and building a life that's yours in every sense. Vulnerability brings freedom, purpose, and connection. It allows you to live with a sense of wholeness, knowing that every part of you is worthy of being seen.

So here's the truth: vulnerability is the bridge between who you are and who you're meant to become. It's the path to living fully, freely, and fearlessly. By choosing vulnerability, you're choosing a life where you can finally be at peace, where you're no longer hiding but standing tall in your own truth. And that, right there, is a life worth living.

# Chapter 11:
# Redefine Success
# on Your Own Terms

Success. It's a word that's been defined for us since we were kids. For most of us, society handed us a formula: success means a good job, a nice house, the right relationships, and a steady paycheck. It's about achievements, milestones, and things you can show off on a resume. But here's the truth most people don't talk about—none of that means a damn thing if it doesn't align with what you want from life. Real success isn't something you can measure by someone else's standards; it's something only you can define. And if you're living by society's blueprint instead of your own, you're never going to feel fulfilled, no matter how many boxes you check off.

Redefining success on your own terms starts with letting go of what you think you "should" want. The pressures of achievement, the comparisons, the need for validation—all of that has been woven into us so deeply that it can feel impossible to break free. But the moment you start questioning it, you realize that a lot of what you thought you wanted was just borrowed from other people's expectations. This isn't about rejecting traditional achievements; it's about making sure they actually matter to you. It's about asking yourself, *Is this what I want, or is this what I think I'm supposed to want?*

One of the first steps to defining success on your own terms is identifying what truly brings you a sense of fulfillment. For some, success might mean financial security, while for others, it could mean creativity, freedom, or time with loved ones. Maybe it's about making a difference, or maybe it's about living simply. Success doesn't have to look the same for everyone, and it doesn't have to be impressive to anyone but you. In fact, the quieter forms of success—the ones that can't be posted on social media or listed on a CV—are often the most meaningful.

Here's a tough truth I had to learn: chasing someone else's version of success only leads to burnout. You spend years working toward goals that don't resonate, pouring yourself into achievements that don't satisfy. And when you finally reach those milestones, you find they're empty because they were never meant for you. This is why it's so crucial to define success for yourself, to figure out what actually makes you feel alive, connected, and purposeful. Maybe it's building something from scratch, or maybe it's finding peace in simplicity. Whatever it is, own it. Your version of success doesn't need to impress anyone but you.

A practical exercise to start redefining success is to make a list of your core values. These are the principles that matter most to you, the things you'd want to be remembered for. Ask yourself questions like, *What makes me feel at peace? What am I doing when I feel most fulfilled? What kind of life do I want to look back on when I'm old?* Your answers to these questions can reveal the areas where success feels most genuine to you. It's about going beyond the surface and getting clear on what genuinely resonates with who you are.

Another key part of redefining success is learning to tune out the noise. Society has a way of shouting its version of success at you from every direction—through media, through family, through friends. But this is your life, and the more you listen to other people's voices, the harder it becomes to hear your own. Set boundaries around what you let influence you. Spend time with people who respect your values, people who aren't obsessed with fitting into the traditional mold, people who are willing to support your unique path. The less you're surrounded by "shoulds" and "musts," the easier it is to see the life that actually feels right for you.

One of the hardest parts of redefining success is accepting that it might mean disappointing others. Maybe your family expected you to follow a certain path, or maybe friends can't understand why you're not interested in what they're chasing. But here's the thing—true success doesn't depend on anyone else's approval. If you're living your life for validation, then it's not really yours. Disappointing others is part of choosing authenticity over acceptance, of honoring your own journey rather than trying to fit into theirs. The people who truly care about you will eventually respect your choices, and those who can't? They weren't meant to walk this path with you.

Redefining success is about choosing freedom. It's choosing to live by your own rules, to follow your own instincts, and to create a life that feels like yours. It might look unconventional, it might be misunderstood, but it will be real. It will be honest. And that's worth more than any amount of external validation.

So here's the truth: success is whatever you decide it is. It doesn't have to be impressive to anyone but you. And when you stop living for someone else's applause, when you stop measuring your life by standards that aren't your own, you find a peace that's priceless. You find that real success isn't a destination; it's a way of living, a choice to honor your own truth every day. And that's something no one can ever take away from you.

One of the most freeing things about defining success on your own terms is realizing that it doesn't have to be big, flashy, or impressive. Real success is often found in the "small" moments—the quiet achievements that others might overlook but that bring you genuine fulfillment. Society loves to celebrate the big wins: promotions, big purchases, accolades. But those are just milestones. Fulfillment, true success, is built on the small, everyday choices that align with who you are. When you can find meaning in the simple things, life starts to feel richer, and the pressure to constantly achieve fades.

In a world that's constantly rushing toward the next big thing, slowing down to appreciate small successes can feel almost rebellious. But these "small" moments are where life actually happens. It's in the satisfaction of finishing a project you care about, even if it's just for yourself. It's in having a meaningful conversation with a friend, in learning something new, or in spending time on something that brings you joy. These moments might not seem monumental, but they're the threads that hold your life together. They're what make your life feel like yours.

When you shift your focus to small successes, you're essentially redefining what "enough" means for you. Instead of chasing after some vague, far-off idea of success, you start recognizing it in your daily life. You realize that "enough" isn't a certain income level, a number of followers, or the size of your home. Enough is having a day where you feel fulfilled, even if it doesn't look like much from the outside. Enough is knowing that you're aligned with your values, that you're spending your time on things that matter to you, not just on things that others value.

One way to start embracing small successes is by practicing daily reflection. At the end of each day, take a moment to acknowledge something you accomplished, something that made you feel connected, or something you're grateful for. It could be as simple as getting out of bed on a hard day, creating something you're proud of, or even just making time for self-care. These reflections remind you that success doesn't have to be huge to be meaningful. Over time, this habit of acknowledging small wins helps you shift your perspective, showing you that fulfillment is already present in your life, even if it doesn't look like the traditional markers of success.

Another powerful approach is to set intentions rather than goals. Goals tend to be outcome-focused, and when they're not achieved, it's easy to feel like you've fallen short. Intentions, on the other hand, are about how you want to live each day. Instead of aiming for a big, end-of-the-road achievement, intentions guide you in the moment. They might look like "I want to approach today with kindness," or "I want to give myself permission to rest." By focusing on intentions, you're giving yourself a way to feel successful every day, regardless of the outcomes. You're creating a life that feels intentional and fulfilling, one that isn't driven by constant need for validation or achievement.

Small successes also mean being present. When you're constantly chasing the next big thing, it's easy to miss what's happening right in front of you. But the most meaningful moments aren't always planned or grand—they're often the spontaneous, everyday experiences that make life feel worth living. When you can be present, you start noticing things you might have overlooked: a sunset, a laugh, a moment of connection. You start to see that success isn't a destination; it's a collection of these moments, an awareness of what's meaningful to you right now, not just what's waiting at some future finish line.

Letting go of the need for big wins doesn't mean you stop striving. It means you start finding value in the process, in the journey itself. Big achievements are still valid, but they're no longer the only thing you live for. You give yourself permission to appreciate the daily steps, the small victories that build a life you're proud of. In doing so, you're no longer waiting for a big break or a massive win to feel successful. You're already successful, because you're living a life that feels good, right now.

Embracing small successes takes the pressure off and brings you back to what really matters. It's a reminder that you don't have to prove anything to anyone, that your life isn't a checklist. When you stop chasing, you find peace in where you are, knowing that success isn't something you're constantly reaching for—it's something you're already living, every day. And when you let go of the need for big wins, you open up space to appreciate the life you've already built, one small success at a time.

For most of us, setbacks feel like failure, like a reason to give up, or worse, a reason to doubt ourselves. Society has trained us to see setbacks as evidence that we're not good enough, not capable, or not meant to succeed. But here's the truth: setbacks aren't signs that you're off track; they're part of the journey. They're proof that you're trying, risking, and learning. If you're going to live by your own definition of success, you have to stop seeing setbacks as failure and start seeing them as the natural stepping stones they are.

Setbacks can teach you more than success ever could. They show you where you're strong, where you need growth, and where you're willing to push beyond your comfort zone. It's easy to be confident when things are going well, but true resilience is built in the moments when things fall apart. When you face a setback and choose to keep going, to find another way, or to learn from it, you're building a kind of strength that no amount of smooth sailing could ever give you.

One way to reframe setbacks is to see them as feedback, not failure. Each time something doesn't go as planned, ask yourself, *What can I learn from this?* or *How can I approach this differently next time?* This approach shifts your focus from self-doubt to self-growth. Instead of internalizing the setback as a flaw in who you are, you see it as an opportunity to adjust, to adapt, and to improve. Failure only becomes permanent if you choose to stop moving forward. If you keep learning and adjusting, each setback just becomes part of the process, a stepping stone toward the version of success that's meant for you.

Another powerful perspective is to embrace setbacks as signs that you're pushing boundaries. If you're constantly succeeding without setbacks, you're probably playing it too safe. Real growth, real progress, happens when you stretch yourself beyond what feels comfortable, and that inevitably involves setbacks. When you're willing to experience them, you're showing yourself that you're not here to settle, that you're committed to growth, to becoming someone stronger, wiser, and more resilient. Setbacks become a badge of courage, proof that you're not holding back.

One of the most transformative things you can do is to change how you talk to yourself when setbacks happen. Instead of falling into self-criticism, practice self-compassion. Remind yourself that setbacks are universal; everyone faces them, even the people you admire. Instead of saying, "I messed up," try saying, "I'm learning." Instead of saying, "I'll never succeed," say, "I'm figuring it out." This shift in language reinforces that setbacks aren't a reflection of your worth; they're simply part of the process. The more compassion you show yourself, the easier it becomes to move forward with confidence, even when things don't go as planned.

A great way to embrace setbacks is to document your journey. Keep a journal or record where you can track your progress, including the moments that didn't go as planned. Write about the setbacks, but also write about what you learned from them, how you adapted, and how you kept going. Over time, you'll see patterns of growth, resilience, and perseverance. You'll see that each setback was just one moment in a much larger journey. This perspective makes setbacks feel smaller, more manageable, and easier to navigate because you're seeing them in the context of your entire journey, not just as isolated failures.

Finally, remind yourself that setbacks don't define your worth. Success isn't about a perfect path; it's about a commitment to keep going. Each time you hit a roadblock and find a way to move past it, you're proving to yourself that you're capable, that you're resourceful, and that you have what it takes to achieve the life you envision. Your worth isn't in your ability to avoid failure; it's in your willingness to face it, to learn from it, and to keep pushing forward.

Embracing setbacks as part of your journey transforms how you approach life. It gives you permission to take risks, to be bold, and to pursue the things that matter to you without the constant fear of "messing up." Setbacks aren't dead ends—they're just detours, redirecting you to a better version of your path. And when you're willing to see them that way, you're no longer held back by fear of failure. You're free to chase your version of success, knowing that each step, each setback, is bringing you closer to who you're meant to be.

Comparison is one of the biggest obstacles to redefining success. We live in a world that constantly bombards us with other people's achievements, curated lives, and highlight reels, making it hard to focus on our own path without feeling like we're somehow falling behind. But here's a hard truth: comparison kills joy. It pulls you out of your own journey, robs you of your unique perspective, and replaces gratitude with envy. If you're going to live by your own definition of success, you have to release the need to measure yourself against anyone else.

The first step to breaking free from comparison is acknowledging that no one else has lived your life, faced your struggles, or walked your path. Your journey is yours alone. And because of that, your version of success will look different from anyone else's. There is no "one size fits all" when it comes to fulfillment. When you compare yourself to others, you're using their lives as a measuring stick for your own, but that stick doesn't fit your unique experiences, challenges, or values. The truth is, no one else's path can ever define yours.

One powerful way to release comparison is to shift your focus inward. Instead of constantly looking at what others are doing, start tuning into your own progress, your own growth, and your own wins. Reflect on where you were a year ago, or even six months ago, and see how far you've come. Recognize the steps you've taken, the lessons you've learned, and the resilience you've built along the way. These reflections remind you that success isn't a race or a competition; it's a journey that you're on for yourself. When you stop looking outward for validation, you start to find peace in your own progress.

Another helpful practice is to express gratitude for what you already have. Comparison thrives on the belief that you need what someone else has to be happy or fulfilled. But gratitude shifts that perspective, grounding you in the present and reminding you of the richness that already exists in your life. Each time you find yourself comparing, pause and list three things you're grateful for. This simple shift breaks the cycle of comparison and brings you back to a place of contentment. Gratitude reminds you that your life, as it is right now, is enough.

It's also important to remember that comparison is often based on illusions. People share what they want others to see, the polished version of their lives. Social media, especially, is a highlight reel, a collection of moments that don't capture the full story. You might be comparing your everyday reality to someone else's best moments, but the truth is, everyone has struggles, doubts, and setbacks. When you let go of the illusions and realize that everyone is dealing with their own challenges, it becomes easier to appreciate your own journey without feeling inadequate.

One of the most freeing things about releasing comparison is that it allows you to celebrate others without feeling diminished. When you're no longer measuring yourself against others, you can genuinely appreciate their successes without feeling like it takes anything away from you. You stop seeing life as a zero-sum game, where someone else's win means your loss. Instead, you see that there's enough success, happiness, and fulfillment to go around. Other people's achievements become a source of inspiration rather than a reason for self-doubt. You're able to support others without losing sight of your own path.

Finally, releasing comparison gives you the space to define success in ways that feel true to you. You're no longer living for applause or approval; you're living for yourself. You're choosing a path that reflects your values, your priorities, and your vision, rather than trying to replicate someone else's. This freedom is priceless, because it allows you to create a life that's deeply fulfilling, even if it doesn't look like anyone else's version of "successful." True success isn't about standing out in a crowd; it's about feeling at peace with who you are and the life you're building.

So here's the bottom line: comparison is a distraction from the life you're meant to live. When you let go of it, you're free to focus on your own journey, to appreciate your own growth, and to build a life that's uniquely yours. True success isn't about keeping up with anyone else; it's about moving forward, one step at a time, in a direction that feels right to you. And when you embrace that freedom, you're no longer limited by anyone else's standards. You're living a life that's authentic, intentional, and fully your own.

# Chapter 12: Choosing Peace Over Perfection

Perfectionism is one of the most exhausting traps we can fall into. It's the relentless belief that if we're just flawless enough—if we say the right things, make no mistakes, achieve everything on the list—then we'll finally be worthy of love, acceptance, or respect. But here's the reality: perfection doesn't exist, and the constant pursuit of it only keeps us from finding peace. When you let go of the need to be perfect, you're giving yourself permission to live, to be real, and to experience life without constantly critiquing yourself. You're choosing peace over an impossible standard that was never meant to define you.

Perfectionism isn't really about being "better"; it's about fear. It's the fear of not being enough, of being judged, of making mistakes that might expose you as less than. But here's what I had to learn: imperfection isn't something to hide or be ashamed of. It's the very thing that makes us human. It's what connects us, what makes us relatable, and what allows us to experience true growth. When you let yourself be imperfect, you're embracing the fullness of who you are, flaws and all, and that kind of acceptance is where real peace lives.

The first step to letting go of perfectionism is recognizing where it shows up in your life. Maybe it's in your work, where you're constantly pushing yourself to outperform, or in relationships, where you try to be the perfect partner, friend, or parent. Maybe it's in the expectations you set for yourself—how you look, how you present yourself, or how you think others perceive you. Identifying these areas is crucial because once you see where perfectionism is driving your actions, you can start challenging it.

One of the most effective ways to combat perfectionism is to practice self-compassion. Instead of criticizing yourself for every perceived flaw, start treating yourself with the same kindness you'd offer a friend. When you make a mistake, instead of tearing yourself down, say, "It's okay. I'm allowed to make mistakes. I'm learning." Self-compassion breaks the cycle of self-criticism and reminds you that you don't have to be perfect to be valuable, that your worth isn't defined by your performance but by who you are as a whole.

Another powerful approach is to focus on progress, not perfection. Rather than striving for flawless results, allow yourself to celebrate small wins, the incremental steps you take along the way. Progress is real, it's meaningful, and it's something you can appreciate right now. Perfection is elusive and distant, a constant moving target that keeps you stuck in dissatisfaction. By choosing progress over perfection, you're acknowledging your effort, your resilience, and your commitment to growth. You're shifting the focus from outcomes to the journey itself, which is where real fulfillment lives.

One practice that's helped me let go of perfectionism is reframing mistakes as learning opportunities. Instead of seeing mistakes as failures, start viewing them as valuable teachers. Every mistake brings insight, showing you what works and what doesn't, what you need to adjust, and how you can grow. When you see mistakes this way, they lose their power to make you feel inadequate. They become part of your journey, something that helps you move forward, rather than something that holds you back. You realize that making mistakes doesn't make you flawed; it makes you human, and there's nothing wrong with that.

A daily practice that helps with releasing perfectionism is embracing "good enough." This doesn't mean you stop trying or that you don't put effort into what matters to you. It means recognizing when you've given your best for the day and allowing that to be enough. If you're constantly chasing an ideal version of everything, you'll never feel at peace. Let yourself stop when something feels good enough, when it feels right in the moment. Over time, this practice becomes a form of self-respect, a way of valuing yourself over the need to prove something. It lets you rest, breathe, and enjoy life without the endless push for more.

Lastly, remind yourself that you don't need to be perfect to be loved, to be respected, or to be happy. People don't connect with perfection—they connect with realness, with vulnerability, with authenticity. When you show up as yourself, imperfections and all, you're giving others permission to do the same. You're creating space for genuine connection, for relationships that don't rely on constant performance but are built on acceptance and honesty. Perfectionism isolates you; authenticity brings you closer to yourself and others.

Choosing peace over perfection isn't about lowering your standards or settling. It's about freeing yourself from an impossible burden, about honoring your worth beyond the need to be flawless. When you let go of perfectionism, you're choosing to live fully, to make mistakes without shame, to grow without constant pressure, and to be exactly who you are. And that, right there, is the most powerful choice you can make.

One of the biggest myths we're taught is that growth is a straight line—a path with clearly marked steps, milestones, and no detours. But real growth? It's messy. It's full of starts and stops, moments of progress mixed with setbacks, times of clarity interrupted by times of doubt. Growth doesn't happen in a perfect, upward trajectory; it happens in loops, spirals, and unexpected turns. And the sooner we accept that, the sooner we can find peace in our journey instead of feeling like we're constantly falling short.

Messy progress isn't a flaw; it's part of the process. There will be days where you feel like you're unstoppable, like you're finally making headway. And then, just as quickly, there will be days where you feel like you're back at square one. This doesn't mean you've failed; it means you're human. Growth is nonlinear because life is nonlinear. Situations change, emotions shift, and progress often involves revisiting old lessons from new perspectives. Embracing the messiness of growth is about understanding that each step, forward or back, is bringing you closer to the person you're meant to become.

One of the most liberating things about accepting messy progress is that it gives you room to breathe. You no longer have to hold yourself to a rigid standard of constant improvement.

Instead, you can allow yourself to evolve in your own time, at your own pace. Growth is deeply personal, and it's not a competition. Some parts of your journey will feel slow, some will feel like breakthroughs, and some might feel like setbacks. But all of it—every confusing, uncertain, frustrating step—is part of the journey.

A practical way to embrace messy progress is to stop looking at things in terms of "success" or "failure." Life isn't a series of pass/fail tests; it's a continuous flow of experiences that shape you. Instead of asking, *Did I succeed or fail?* try asking, *What did I learn? How did I grow?* This shift in perspective lets you appreciate the process itself, even if things didn't turn out as planned. It allows you to see each experience as valuable, even if it wasn't perfect.

Another powerful way to embrace imperfect growth is to reflect on how far you've come, rather than only focusing on how far you still want to go. When you're constantly looking at what you haven't achieved, it's easy to feel discouraged. But when you look back and recognize the steps you've taken, the lessons you've learned, and the resilience you've built, you start to see that progress is real, even if it's messy. Reflecting on your journey reminds you that growth isn't about reaching a destination; it's about who you're becoming along the way.

Messy progress also means letting go of the idea that there's a "right" way to do things. Maybe you have days where you don't feel motivated, days where you struggle to stick to routines, or days where you feel lost. That's okay. Growth isn't about ticking boxes or following a perfect plan; it's about showing up as best as you can in each moment. It's about honoring where you are, even if it's not where you thought you'd be. When you let go of the idea that you need to be constantly "on track," you give yourself permission to grow in a way that feels authentic and sustainable.

Accepting messy progress is also about releasing the fear of judgment. Sometimes, we hold back from trying new things or taking risks because we're afraid of how we'll look if we don't get it right. But the truth is, people who matter won't judge you for trying and failing; they'll respect you for your courage. The people who love and support you won't mind if your path looks a little different from theirs, or if your journey takes a few detours. Letting go of the need to appear perfect allows you to live more fully, to explore, to take chances, and to grow without constantly worrying about how you're being perceived.

Ultimately, messy progress is a reminder that life isn't about perfection—it's about presence. It's about being present in the moment, even when things feel chaotic, uncertain, or difficult. When you embrace the mess, you're choosing to find beauty in the journey, to celebrate the small wins, to accept the setbacks, and to trust that each moment is leading you somewhere meaningful. Growth isn't about doing it perfectly; it's about doing it authentically, flaws and all.

So here's the truth: growth is messy because life is messy. And that's okay. You don't need a perfect path to become who you're meant to be. You just need the courage to keep moving forward, to learn from each experience, and to trust that the journey—messy as it may be—is exactly what you need. When you let go of perfection and embrace the mess, you're choosing a life that's real, a life that's honest, and a life that's fully, unapologetically yours.

Self-compassion is the foundation of finding peace in an imperfect life. When things go sideways, when you make a mistake, or when you face a setback, it's easy to turn against yourself. Society has conditioned us to believe that mistakes are something to be ashamed of, that every misstep reflects a flaw in who we are. But if you're going to choose peace over perfection, self-compassion has to become your default. It's the practice of treating yourself with kindness instead of criticism, with understanding instead of judgment. It's the difference between feeling broken by a setback and seeing it as just another part of the journey.

Self-compassion isn't about making excuses or ignoring your own responsibility. It's about acknowledging that you're human, that you're learning, and that mistakes don't define your worth. They're part of the process, part of being alive. When you can show up for yourself with the same empathy you'd show a friend, you start building resilience. You're no longer breaking yourself down over every misstep; you're using them as opportunities to grow, to reflect, and to move forward with more wisdom.

One of the first steps in practicing self-compassion is changing the way you talk to yourself. When you make a mistake or face a setback, notice the tone of your inner voice. Are you quick to criticize, to call yourself names, to dwell on what you should have done differently? If so, take a moment to pause and ask yourself, *Would I talk to someone else like this?* If the answer is no, then it's time to reframe your self-talk. Try saying, *It's okay to make mistakes; I'm still learning,* or *This setback doesn't define me; it's just a part of my growth.* Shifting your self-talk from criticism to kindness might feel unnatural at first, but with practice, it becomes a habit that builds self-worth rather than tearing it down.

Another way to practice self-compassion is by giving yourself permission to rest. Perfectionism often comes with a relentless drive to keep pushing, to achieve more, to "fix" everything. But peace doesn't come from constantly pushing; it comes from allowing yourself to pause. If you're exhausted, overwhelmed, or dealing with a setback, give yourself the space to recharge without guilt. Rest is not laziness; it's a necessary part of growth. When you allow yourself to rest, you're showing yourself that you're worthy of care, that you deserve to be nurtured, even in moments when you don't feel at your best.

Self-compassion also means letting go of the need to have all the answers. Sometimes, the hardest part of facing setbacks is the feeling of being lost, of not knowing what to do next. But self-compassion is about accepting that uncertainty is a natural part of growth. You don't have to have everything figured out; you just need to take one step at a time. Remind yourself that it's okay not to know all the answers, that you're allowed to learn as you go. This acceptance takes the pressure off, giving you room to explore, to make mistakes, and to trust that clarity will come in time.

A practical exercise for self-compassion is to create a "Self-Kindness Journal." Each day, write down something kind that you can say to yourself, especially when things aren't going as planned. This might be as simple as, "I'm proud of myself for trying," or "Today was tough, but I'm doing my best." This journal serves as a reminder of the kindness you deserve, especially on days when self-doubt tries to take over. Over time, it becomes a record of your growth, a source of comfort when setbacks come, and a tool to help you rebuild your confidence.

Finally, self-compassion means forgiving yourself for the past. We all have moments we wish we could undo, choices we'd make differently if we had the chance. But holding onto regret only keeps you stuck. Self-compassion is about choosing to let go, to say, "I did the best I could with what I knew at the time." Forgiving yourself doesn't mean you're excusing mistakes; it means you're freeing yourself from the weight of them. You're allowing yourself to move forward with less baggage, more grace, and the understanding that growth is messy, imperfect, and beautifully human.

Choosing peace over perfection is an act of self-compassion. It's a commitment to treat yourself with kindness, to show up for yourself even when things are hard, and to understand that setbacks don't define you. They're just chapters in a much bigger story, a story that's uniquely yours. By practicing self-compassion, you're creating a life where you're not just surviving; you're thriving, one imperfect step at a time. And that's where true peace lies—not in the absence of mistakes, but in the presence of acceptance.

True peace doesn't come from reaching a state of perfection; it comes from reaching a state of acceptance. It's the ability to look at yourself—your past, your present, your flaws, and your strengths—and say, *I am enough.* When you're rooted in acceptance, you're no longer living with a constant need to prove yourself, to fix every perceived flaw, or to meet impossible standards. Instead, you're giving yourself the gift of being okay with who you are, exactly as you are.

Acceptance doesn't mean you stop growing or striving. It means you recognize that you're already worthy, that you're already whole, even as you continue to evolve. It's about understanding that there's a difference between self-improvement and self-acceptance. Self-improvement says, "I need to be better to be worthy." Self-acceptance says, "I'm already worthy, and I'm growing because I want to, not because I have to." Acceptance creates a foundation of inner peace that no amount of achievement or validation from others can match.

One of the first steps to building a life rooted in acceptance is to acknowledge and embrace your flaws. We all have parts of ourselves that we wish were different—habits we're working to change, past mistakes, quirks that make us feel insecure. But here's the truth: those flaws are part of what makes you uniquely you. Embracing them doesn't mean you're settling; it means you're choosing to see yourself as a whole person, worthy of love and respect just as you are. When you can say, "I accept myself, flaws and all," you're releasing the pressure to be someone you're not, and that freedom is invaluable.

Another powerful aspect of acceptance is learning to be present. Often, we live in a constant state of "next"—what's next to accomplish, the next goal, the next version of ourselves. But peace is found in the now, in the present moment. Practice grounding yourself in what's happening right here, right now. Whether you're sitting with a friend, working on a project, or simply taking a walk, remind yourself that this moment is enough. You don't need to constantly improve or fix anything to make it meaningful. The more you practice presence, the easier it becomes to accept each moment—and yourself—just as you are.

Building a life rooted in acceptance also means letting go of comparisons. When you accept yourself, you're no longer measuring your worth against others. You're no longer striving to fit a mold that wasn't designed for you. Instead, you're living in alignment with who you are, honoring your own pace, your own path, and your own growth. Comparison fades when you're grounded in self-acceptance, because you understand that your worth isn't tied to how you stack up against someone else; it's tied to how true you are to yourself.

One practice that fosters acceptance is the habit of daily gratitude—not just for things around you, but for who you are. Each day, take a moment to express gratitude for something you appreciate about yourself. Maybe it's your resilience, your creativity, your ability to make others laugh, or simply the fact that you keep showing up, day after day. This practice shifts your focus from what you wish was different to what you're proud of, building a foundation of acceptance that makes you feel whole.

Lastly, acceptance is about allowing yourself to experience life fully, without constantly analyzing or judging. When you're at peace with who you are, you're more open to whatever life brings, because you're no longer trying to control or perfect every outcome. You can enjoy moments of happiness without wondering if you deserve them. You can face challenges without letting them define your worth. And you can let life be messy, because you know that messiness doesn't take away from your value. You're no longer striving to be "enough" because you already know that you are.

Choosing peace over perfection is an ongoing journey. It's a commitment to honoring your own worth, to treating yourself with kindness, and to living in a way that feels authentic and true. Acceptance is a daily choice, a way of grounding yourself in the belief that you're already whole. When you live with acceptance, you're creating a life where peace is a constant, not a destination. You're free to grow, to make mistakes, to be real, and to find joy in the imperfect beauty of your own journey.

Because here's the truth: peace isn't found in a perfect life. It's found in a life that's loved and accepted, exactly as it is. And that kind of life, rooted in acceptance, is the greatest gift you can give yourself.

# Chapter 13: The Power of Letting Go

We often carry so much that no longer serves us—old grudges, outdated beliefs, toxic relationships, self-doubt, and even expectations that we never agreed to in the first place. Letting go isn't just a choice; it's a powerful act of self-respect. It's about giving yourself permission to stop holding onto the things that drain you, hurt you, or keep you stuck in cycles that you've outgrown. When you release what no longer serves you, you're creating space for growth, for joy, and for the life you actually want to live.

Letting go isn't about forgetting or pretending the past didn't happen. It's about acknowledging what's no longer helpful or fulfilling and making the decision to release it. It's about recognizing that you have the right to set down any burden that doesn't align with the person you're becoming. Sometimes, we hold onto things out of habit or even out of a sense of loyalty to who we once were. But just because something was part of your past doesn't mean it has to be part of your future.

One of the first steps to letting go is identifying what's taking up space in your life. Start by asking yourself, *What am I hold-*

*ing onto that no longer serves me?* This could be a relationship that's become one-sided, a belief that keeps you from trying new things, or even a habit that drains your energy. Write it all down. Seeing these things on paper can be a powerful reminder of how much you're carrying and what's worth keeping. Once you have a clear picture, you can start making intentional choices about what stays and what goes.

A key part of letting go is learning to set boundaries. Often, we hold onto things because we don't want to disappoint others or we're afraid of judgment. But boundaries aren't about pushing people away; they're about honoring your own needs. Setting boundaries allows you to protect your energy and make space for things that actually bring you fulfillment. If a relationship, a commitment, or even a pattern of behavior is no longer serving you, it's okay to set a boundary. It's okay to say, "This isn't right for me anymore." Boundaries are acts of self-respect, a way of saying that you value your own well-being.

Another part of letting go is releasing the need for closure. Sometimes, we hold onto things because we're waiting for an apology, an explanation, or a sense of finality that may never come. But true closure doesn't come from someone else's words; it comes from within. You don't need someone else to validate your experience or make sense of it for you. Letting go is about accepting that certain things won't be resolved and choosing to move forward anyway. Closure is a choice, a decision to stop waiting and to give yourself permission to heal.

One helpful practice for letting go is visualization. Imagine the things you're holding onto as physical weights, like rocks you're carrying in a backpack. Visualize each thing you want to let go of—an old grudge, a fear, a relationship that no longer aligns—and imagine yourself setting it down, piece by piece. Feel the weight lifting as you let go. This practice reminds you that you have the power to choose what you carry and what you leave behind. Each time you set down a weight, you're creating space for something new, something that aligns with who you are becoming.

Letting go also requires self-compassion. You may find that you're holding onto guilt, regret, or self-criticism from past choices. But holding onto those things only keeps you tied to a version of yourself that you've already outgrown. Practice forgiving yourself for what happened, for the choices you made with the knowledge you had at the time. Letting go isn't just about releasing others; it's about freeing yourself. Self-compassion is a reminder that you're allowed to move forward, that you're worthy of peace, and that you deserve to live without the weight of past mistakes.

As you let go of what no longer serves you, you're making room for new possibilities. You're creating a life that isn't filled with what you've outgrown, but with things that align with who you are now. Letting go isn't a loss; it's a gain. It's reclaiming space for joy, for growth, and for the relationships and experiences that truly resonate with you. You're choosing a life where every part of it feels intentional, meaningful, and reflective of the person you're becoming.

Because here's the truth: you don't have to carry everything. You have the right to set down what no longer serves you, to make space for what does. Letting go isn't easy, but it's powerful. It's a choice to live fully, to let joy in, and to move forward with a heart that's open, not weighed down. And that, right there, is the foundation of a life that's free.

Letting go of control can be one of the hardest things to do, especially if you've been through experiences that taught you to hold on tightly just to feel safe. Control gives us a false sense of security, a belief that if we just try hard enough, plan enough, or worry enough, we can keep life from taking us places we don't want to go. But the truth is, control is an illusion. No matter how much we try to micromanage every outcome, life will always throw the unexpected our way. Real peace comes not from controlling everything, but from learning to trust in the flow of life and letting go of the need to control every detail.

At its core, the need for control is rooted in fear—fear of uncertainty, fear of failure, fear of the unknown. Control feels like a way to protect ourselves from disappointment or pain, but it actually does the opposite. When we try to control everything, we limit our ability to experience life as it is. We close ourselves off to opportunities, to growth, and to moments of joy that don't fit our plans. By letting go of control, we're giving ourselves permission to live more freely, to embrace the beauty of spontaneity, and to open up to the experiences that life has in store for us.

One of the first steps to releasing control is shifting your mindset from *What if something goes wrong?* to *What if things turn out even better than I could have planned?* It's easy to get caught up in worst-case scenarios, but these thoughts are often just fear in disguise. Remind yourself that life has a way of working things out, sometimes in ways you couldn't anticipate. Letting go of control doesn't mean you stop caring or that you stop trying. It means you start trusting that things can unfold in ways you didn't expect, that not everything needs to be perfectly planned for it to turn out okay.

A practical approach to letting go of control is to start with small things. Try practicing what I call "intentional surrender" in everyday situations. For example, if you're worried about an outcome at work, give it your best effort, and then intentionally release the need to micromanage every detail. Remind yourself that you've done what you can, and that the rest is out of your hands. This practice builds your trust in the process and reminds you that you can handle whatever comes next, even if it doesn't go exactly as planned. Small acts of letting go help you build the courage to release control in larger, more challenging areas of your life.

Another essential part of releasing control is embracing uncertainty. We often cling to control because we're uncomfortable with the unknown, but uncertainty is a natural part of life. When you can make peace with not knowing exactly how things will turn out, you're giving yourself permission to live in the present rather than constantly worrying about the future. Practice accepting uncertainty as part of the journey, a part that holds possibilities and potential you might never have imagined. By letting go of the need to know everything, you create room for life to surprise you in positive ways.

Letting go of control also means releasing perfectionism. Often, we try to control things because we're afraid of making mistakes, of falling short, or of being seen as imperfect. But when you release the need to control, you're giving yourself permission to be human. You're allowing yourself to make mistakes, to learn as you go, and to grow through experience rather than from a place of constant planning. Life doesn't need to be perfect for it to be meaningful. In fact, some of the most beautiful moments are the unplanned ones, the ones that happen when you're least expecting it.

One practice that can help with letting go of control is to focus on your intentions rather than specific outcomes. Instead of fixating on how things should turn out, think about the kind of energy you want to bring into each situation. Set an intention to show up with openness, kindness, or resilience, regardless of the outcome. This shift in focus gives you a sense of purpose without the pressure to control every detail. It reminds you that the journey itself is valuable, that the process matters just as much as the destination.

Finally, letting go of control requires trust—trust in yourself, trust in the process, and trust in life itself. Remind yourself of times when things worked out, even when they didn't go according to plan. Trust that you have the resilience to handle whatever comes, and that sometimes, life's unexpected turns lead to the best outcomes. Trust doesn't mean that everything will be easy or that things will always go smoothly. It means you're willing to face whatever comes, knowing that you'll grow from it, adapt to it, and ultimately find a way through it.

Letting go of control isn't about giving up or being passive. It's about embracing life as it is, without needing to manipulate every outcome. It's about finding peace in the present moment, trusting yourself to navigate the unknown, and knowing that you don't need to have everything figured out to live a life that's fulfilling and meaningful. When you release control, you're freeing yourself to experience life fully, to flow with its rhythm, and to discover joy in places you never expected.

Because here's the truth: life isn't meant to be controlled—it's meant to be lived. And when you choose to trust the journey instead of trying to control every step, you're choosing freedom, peace, and a life that's open to possibility.

We all carry stories about ourselves, narratives shaped by past experiences, traumas, and beliefs we've internalized over time. These stories tell us who we are, what we're capable of, and what we deserve. But here's the thing: many of these stories are outdated, inaccurate, and even harmful. They were created during times when we didn't have the insight or perspective we do now. Letting go of these old stories is an essential part of growth—it's about choosing to release the narratives that no longer serve us and creating space for new, empowering ones that do.

Our stories are often based on past wounds. Maybe you were told that you weren't smart enough, strong enough, or worthy enough, and over time, you started to believe it. Or maybe certain experiences taught you that life is harsh, that relationships are unsafe, or that success is always out of reach. These stories become mental scripts that play on repeat, shaping the way we see ourselves and the choices we make. Letting go of these stories is about acknowledging that they're just that—stories. They're not absolute truths, and they don't have to define you anymore.

The first step in releasing old stories is recognizing them for what they are. Start by paying attention to the beliefs that limit you, the thoughts that pop up when you're about to try something new, or the doubts that creep in when you're stepping out of your comfort zone. Ask yourself, *Where did this belief come from? Who or what taught me to think this way?* Often, just identifying the origin of a belief helps you realize that it doesn't truly belong to you; it's something you picked up along the way, something you've outgrown.

Once you've identified these limiting beliefs, challenge them. Question their validity. If your old story says, *I'm not good enough to succeed,* ask yourself, *Is that really true? What evidence do I have to the contrary?* Start listing your strengths, your past accomplishments, and the times when you've proven yourself capable. Challenging these stories doesn't erase them overnight, but it begins to weaken their grip on you. Over time, you start to see that these beliefs are just echoes from the past, not reflections of who you are today.

One powerful way to rewrite your narrative is through affirmations. Begin by crafting affirmations that counteract the old stories. For instance, if you've carried the belief, *I'm always going to be alone,* try affirming, *I am worthy of love and meaningful connection.* If you've believed, *I'm not capable of success,* replace it with, *I have the resilience and skills to achieve my goals.* Write these affirmations down, repeat them daily, and let them sink in. They're not just empty words; they're seeds of a new story, a story that's rooted in possibility rather than limitation.

Another practice for releasing old stories is visualization. Imagine your life without the limits of these old narratives. Picture yourself living without the fear, without the self-doubt, without the weight of past beliefs. See yourself as the person you're becoming—confident, resilient, and free. Visualization isn't about pretending your problems don't exist; it's about giving yourself permission to imagine a new reality. When you start visualizing a different story, you're telling your mind that change is possible, that you don't have to stay bound by the limitations of the past.

Forgiving yourself and others is also a powerful tool in releasing old stories. Often, our narratives are tied to pain or betrayal from the past. Maybe someone hurt you, or maybe you made choices you regret. Holding onto that pain only keeps you stuck in the old story, reliving the hurt over and over. Forgiveness doesn't mean you're excusing what happened; it means you're releasing its hold on you. When you forgive, you're choosing to set yourself free from the weight of the past, to let go of the resentment or guilt that keeps you tethered to an outdated narrative.

Finally, surround yourself with people who support the new story you're creating. It's hard to rewrite your narrative when you're surrounded by people who reinforce the old one. Seek out relationships that encourage your growth, people who see your potential and value your journey. Let them reflect back to you the qualities and strengths you might not always see in yourself. When you're around people who support your evolution, it becomes easier to let go of old stories and embrace the person you're becoming.

Letting go of old stories isn't about erasing the past; it's about choosing to write a new future. It's about saying, "I am not defined by where I've been; I'm defined by where I'm going." Each time you challenge an old belief, each time you affirm your worth, you're taking another step toward freedom. You're choosing to live a life that's shaped not by fear, but by possibility. And that's the power of letting go—it's the freedom to be who you truly are, without the limitations of who you once thought you had to be.

Letting go isn't always about small adjustments or breaking old habits; sometimes, it's about saying goodbye. Whether it's a relationship, a job, a friendship, or even a dream, some things simply reach a point where they're no longer aligned with who you are or where you're going. Endings are hard because they force us to confront change, uncertainty, and often a deep sense of loss. But they also open up space for something new, something truer to the person you're becoming. When you make peace with endings, you're choosing to honor the past without letting it define your future.

Endings can feel like failure, especially when we've poured time, energy, and emotion into something that no longer works. It's easy to fall into self-doubt, questioning whether you could have done more, tried harder, or been different. But here's the truth: not every ending is a failure. Sometimes, the best thing you can do for yourself is to let go and allow change to happen. Some chapters are meant to close so that new ones can begin, and holding onto something out of fear or guilt only keeps you from experiencing the freedom and growth that await you.

One of the first steps in making peace with an ending is to acknowledge the role it played in your life. Each experience, even the painful or challenging ones, brings lessons. Take a moment to reflect on what this chapter taught you, on the ways it shaped you, and on the growth it sparked. Acknowledging the value of the experience doesn't mean you're denying the pain; it means you're choosing to see both sides. Gratitude for the lessons allows you to move on without bitterness or regret, carrying the growth forward while leaving the heaviness behind.

Another essential part of accepting endings is giving yourself permission to grieve. Letting go is often accompanied by a sense of loss, and that's normal. You're not only saying goodbye to the person, situation, or phase itself; you're also letting go of the hopes, plans, and dreams that came with it. Grieving is part of the process, a way of honoring what once was. Allow yourself to feel sadness, nostalgia, or even anger without judging those emotions. By letting yourself grieve, you're acknowledging the depth of what this chapter meant to you, which ultimately makes it easier to release.

As you let go, it's also important to focus on what you're moving toward, not just what you're leaving behind. When you dwell solely on the loss, it's easy to feel stuck. Shift your focus to the possibilities that this ending creates. Ask yourself, *What am I making space for? What new experiences, relationships, or goals can I pursue now that I'm moving on?* Endings are beginnings in disguise, and they often bring opportunities for growth and self-discovery that you couldn't see when you were still holding on. By looking forward, you're choosing to embrace the freedom that comes from letting go, a freedom that opens the door to new paths and fresh starts.

One powerful practice for moving on is creating a ritual of release. This could be as simple as writing a letter to the person, situation, or version of yourself that you're leaving behind. Pour everything you're feeling into it—the gratitude, the pain, the hopes you once had. Then, when you're ready, let it go. Burn it, bury it, or release it in a way that feels meaningful to you. Rituals give closure to your emotions, providing a tangible way to release what no longer serves you and affirm your commitment to moving forward.

Letting go of the past also means letting go of guilt. Sometimes, we hold onto people or situations out of a sense of obligation, fearing that moving on means we're betraying someone or something. But staying out of guilt is a form of self-betrayal. Remember that you have the right to choose what's best for you, even if others don't understand or agree. Moving on doesn't mean you didn't care or that it wasn't meaningful; it means you're choosing to honor your own path, and that's a choice you're allowed to make without shame.

Lastly, making peace with endings requires trust—trust in yourself and in life's ability to bring you what you need when you need it. Sometimes, we hold on because we're afraid of what will happen if we let go. But true freedom comes from trusting that endings are not empty spaces; they're spaces waiting to be filled with something better suited for where you're going. Trust that as you let go, you're creating room for new connections, new growth, and a life that's even more aligned with who you are now.

Embracing endings doesn't mean you're turning your back on the past; it means you're opening yourself to the future. It's about acknowledging that some things are meant to be cherished, learned from, and then released. When you make peace with endings, you're choosing to let go of what no longer serves you, to honor your journey, and to move forward with hope, resilience, and the understanding that the best is yet to come.

Because here's the truth: letting go isn't about loss—it's about freedom. And when you embrace that freedom, you're allowing life to bring you the next chapter, a chapter that holds the growth, joy, and fulfillment you've been waiting for.

# Chapter 14: Redefining Love and Connection

We hear it all the time: *"Love yourself first."* But self-love isn't just a nice idea or a trendy mantra; it's essential. Self-love is the foundation of every healthy relationship you'll ever have, the starting point for understanding your own needs, setting boundaries, and connecting authentically with others. When you truly love yourself, you're no longer seeking someone else to complete you, validate you, or make you feel worthy. Instead, you're bringing a whole, grounded self to every relationship. Without self-love, connections can quickly become a source of anxiety, insecurity, and dependency. With it, they become a space of mutual respect, honesty, and fulfillment.

Loving yourself first doesn't mean you're putting yourself above others in a selfish way. It means you're honoring yourself enough to show up as you are, to communicate openly, and to accept love without feeling like you have to constantly prove your worth. Self-love builds resilience, gives you the strength to walk away from what doesn't serve you, and allows you to see relationships as a source of joy, not validation. When you love yourself, you're no longer afraid to be alone, because you know you're whole on your own. You're choosing connections based on mutual respect, not out of fear or need.

The first step to practicing self-love is to get to know yourself. That might sound simple, but many of us go through life without really tuning into our own needs, values, and desires. We're so focused on meeting the expectations of others that we lose sight of what genuinely brings us joy, peace, or fulfillment. Start by spending time alone, reflecting on what makes you feel alive, what makes you feel calm, and what truly matters to you. Journaling, meditation, and self-reflection are powerful tools for this. The more you get to know yourself, the easier it becomes to make choices that honor who you are.

Self-love also means treating yourself with kindness. Notice how you talk to yourself, especially in difficult moments. Are you quick to judge, to criticize, or to doubt? If so, practice replacing those harsh words with compassion. Instead of saying, "I messed up again," try saying, "I'm learning, and that's okay." Self-compassion isn't about making excuses; it's about accepting yourself as you are, mistakes and all. When you treat yourself with kindness, you're building a relationship with yourself based on trust and understanding. This self-compassion then becomes the blueprint for how you allow others to treat you.

A big part of self-love is setting boundaries. It's easy to believe that if we just give enough, bend enough, or compromise enough, we'll finally earn love. But real love doesn't require constant sacrifice or self-abandonment. Setting boundaries is an act of self-love that communicates, "I value myself, and I respect myself." Boundaries aren't walls; they're guidelines for healthy relationships. They allow you to show up fully while also protecting your energy, your peace, and your well-being. When you set boundaries, you're teaching others how to treat you, and you're reinforcing that your needs matter, too.

Self-love also means embracing your own worth, independent of external validation. Too often, we look to others to tell us we're good enough, attractive enough, or worthy enough. But self-love is about recognizing your own value, regardless of outside opinions. It's about understanding that your worth isn't defined by your relationship status, your appearance, or anyone else's approval. Practice reminding yourself that you are enough, just as you are, and that your value isn't contingent on what anyone else thinks. This inner confidence makes you less dependent on others' validation, allowing you to approach relationships from a place of strength and security.

A powerful exercise for building self-love is to make a "Self-Appreciation List." Each day, write down one thing you appreciate about yourself. It could be something small, like your sense of humor, or something bigger, like your resilience through tough times. Over time, this list becomes a reminder of your unique qualities and strengths, a way to reinforce that you are worthy of love, from yourself and from others. This practice isn't about arrogance; it's about recognizing the value you bring into the world, which lays the foundation for loving connections with others.

Loving yourself first means you're no longer afraid of being alone. You're no longer settling for half-hearted connections or relationships that drain you. You're choosing connections that enhance your life, that bring you joy, and that align with your values. When you love yourself, you're able to show up as your authentic self, without the need to impress, conform, or shrink.

You're free to build relationships that are rooted in mutual respect, honesty, and acceptance.

Because here's the truth: the most fulfilling relationships are the ones where two whole people come together, not to complete each other, but to share their completeness. When you love yourself first, you're choosing to live fully, to connect deeply, and to let love be a source of joy, not validation. Self-love isn't just the foundation of healthy relationships; it's the foundation of a life that's free, meaningful, and profoundly connected.

Healthy connections don't just happen; they're built intentionally over time. They're based on mutual respect, trust, and honesty—qualities that allow both people to feel safe, valued, and seen. In a world where relationships are often treated as disposable, building healthy connections requires a commitment to depth, to authenticity, and to honoring the needs of everyone involved. It's about creating a space where both people can show up fully, without the fear of being judged, controlled, or misunderstood. Healthy connections are about thriving together, not just surviving.

The foundation of any healthy connection is respect. Respect means honoring each other's individuality, values, and boundaries. It's understanding that you don't have to agree on everything to respect one another, that each person has their own journey, their own experiences, and their own needs. Respect allows space for differences, for individuality, and for growth. It means you're not trying to control or change the other person; you're accepting them as they are, and they're doing the same for you. When respect is present, both people feel valued for who they truly are.

Another pillar of healthy connections is honesty. Honesty creates a relationship built on truth, not pretense. It's about being open about your feelings, your needs, and your boundaries, even when it's uncomfortable. Honesty isn't about brutal truth or hurting someone's feelings; it's about communicating openly with kindness. When you're honest in a relationship, you're giving the other person a clear understanding of who you are and what you need, creating a connection that's grounded in authenticity. Honesty helps you navigate misunderstandings, resolve conflicts, and build a relationship where both people feel safe to be themselves.

Trust is also essential in any healthy connection. Trust isn't built overnight; it's established over time through consistent actions, transparency, and reliability. Trust means you can rely on each other, that you feel secure in each other's presence, and that you don't have to constantly question the other person's intentions. In a relationship built on trust, both people know they can count on each other, not only in good times but especially in difficult ones. Trust allows both people to open up without fear, to lean on each other, and to grow without feeling judged or unsupported.

A practical way to build healthy connections is to practice active listening. Often, we're so focused on what we're going to say next that we miss the chance to truly hear the other person. Active listening means putting your own thoughts aside and being fully present. It's about listening not only to the words being said but to the feelings behind them. When you listen with empathy and curiosity, you're showing the other person that you value their perspective, that their voice matters to you. This kind of listening strengthens the bond and builds a foundation of understanding and compassion.

Boundaries are another critical part of building healthy connections. Boundaries aren't barriers; they're guidelines that protect each person's well-being. Setting boundaries allows you to express what's okay and what's not okay, creating a relationship where both people feel safe and respected. For instance, if you need alone time to recharge, communicate that clearly rather than expecting the other person to intuit it. Boundaries prevent misunderstandings and resentment, ensuring that each person's needs are acknowledged and honored. In a healthy relationship, boundaries are respected without guilt or manipulation; they're a way of showing mutual care.

Conflict resolution is also essential for healthy connections. No relationship is without conflict, but it's how you handle conflict that matters. In healthy connections, both people approach disagreements with a mindset of resolution, not blame. Instead of escalating arguments, they focus on understanding each other's perspectives, finding common ground, and working toward a solution. Conflict can actually strengthen a relationship when it's handled with respect, patience, and empathy. Healthy connections are built by facing challenges together, not by avoiding them or holding grudges.

Finally, healthy connections are nurtured by appreciation. Showing gratitude for each other's presence, for the small acts of kindness, and for the support you receive reinforces the bond. Appreciation isn't just about grand gestures; it's about acknowledging each other's contributions, recognizing the value each person brings, and expressing gratitude regularly. When both people feel appreciated, they're more likely to continue investing in the relationship, building a connection that's fulfilling for both.

Healthy connections are about growth, support, and shared joy. They allow each person to become the best version of themselves while being fully accepted and valued. When a relationship is built on respect, honesty, and trust, it becomes a source of strength, a space where both people can thrive. You're no longer seeking love as a way to fill a void; you're building love as a way to enhance your life, to experience joy, and to share a journey that's meaningful and real.

Because here's the truth: healthy connections are about partnership, not possession. They're about choosing each other, not out of fear, but out of mutual respect, admiration, and a commitment to growth. When you create relationships based on these principles, you're building connections that last, relationships that don't drain you but instead lift you higher.

Not every relationship is meant to last, and not every connection is good for your well-being. Some relationships drain you, undermine your confidence, or keep you stuck in cycles of negativity. Letting go of toxic relationships is one of the most powerful acts of self-love. It's about choosing peace, honoring your worth, and surrounding yourself with people who uplift you rather than weigh you down. Ending a toxic relationship isn't easy, but it's necessary if you're committed to living a life of self-respect and growth.

Toxic relationships can look different for everyone. Sometimes, it's the constant criticism, the subtle manipulations, or the feeling that you're always giving more than you're getting. Other times, it's the realization that you're losing parts of yourself just to keep the peace or to gain approval. Toxic relationships often leave you feeling drained, insecure, and unsure of your own value. They rob you of energy, making it difficult to focus on the people and experiences that genuinely fulfill you.

One of the first steps to letting go of toxic relationships is recognizing the signs. Pay attention to how you feel around certain people. Do you feel uplifted and supported, or do you feel anxious, judged, or belittled? Healthy relationships make you feel valued, while toxic ones make you question your worth. Trust your instincts; if something feels off, it usually is. Acknowledge these feelings without judgment, and remind yourself that you have the right to choose the relationships that serve your well-being.

Setting boundaries is crucial in dealing with toxic relationships. Sometimes, you may not be able to completely distance yourself from a toxic person, especially if it's a family member or someone in your work environment. In these cases, boundaries become your best form of protection. Boundaries allow you to limit the impact that person has on your mental and emotional health. Be clear about what you will and won't tolerate, and don't be afraid to enforce those boundaries, even if it feels uncomfortable. Protecting your peace is more important than keeping others comfortable.

Letting go of toxic relationships also requires self-compassion. Ending a relationship can bring up feelings of guilt, self-doubt, or even grief. You may worry about hurting the other person, or you may fear judgment from others. But self-compassion reminds you that you're not responsible for managing everyone else's feelings. You're allowed to prioritize your well-being. Give yourself permission to feel whatever emotions come up, but don't let guilt keep you tied to relationships that harm you. Choosing to walk away from toxicity is a courageous act of self-respect.

A powerful tool for moving on from toxic relationships is forgiveness—not for the other person's sake, but for yours. Forgiving doesn't mean condoning their behavior or letting them back into your life; it means releasing the anger or resentment that might be holding you back. Carrying that weight only keeps you tethered to the past. By forgiving, you're freeing yourself to move forward without bitterness, allowing yourself to heal and focus on building healthy, positive connections.

It's also essential to fill the space left by a toxic relationship with self-care and supportive connections. Ending a toxic relationship can leave a void, and it's natural to feel lonely or uncertain at first. Use this time to focus on yourself, to rebuild your confidence, and to surround yourself with people who bring positivity and joy into your life. Spend time on activities that make you feel whole, that remind you of your strengths, and that restore your sense of peace. As you prioritize self-care, you're reinforcing that you're worthy of respect, that your happiness matters, and that you deserve relationships rooted in mutual support.

One way to stay grounded as you move on is to write a list of qualities you want in your relationships. Think about what matters most to you—trust, respect, kindness, honesty—and use this list as a guide for choosing future connections. By being clear about your standards, you're less likely to settle for relationships that don't honor your worth. You're choosing to build a circle of people who reflect your values, who appreciate you, and who make you feel safe and respected.

Letting go of toxic relationships doesn't mean you're giving up on people; it means you're prioritizing your well-being. It's about choosing relationships that nourish you, that support your growth, and that make you feel valued. It's about understanding that you deserve a life filled with healthy connections, where you're celebrated rather than diminished. When you let go of what no longer serves you, you're creating space for the relationships that do.

Because here's the truth: you don't have to stay in relationships that hurt you just because you've known the person a long time or because you're afraid of being alone. Letting go is a sign of strength, not weakness. It's a choice to honor yourself, to protect your peace, and to create a life where love and connection uplift you. And when you let go of toxicity, you're making room for a life filled with genuine, nourishing, and joyful relationships.

Vulnerability is the heart of true connection. It's the willingness to be open, to be seen as you are, and to allow others to see you without the masks or the defenses. But vulnerability can feel risky. It means exposing parts of yourself that aren't always perfect, sharing your fears, your dreams, your mistakes, and trusting that the other person will hold that space with care. Yet, without vulnerability, relationships remain shallow, stuck in the realm of surface-level interactions. Embracing vulnerability isn't about oversharing or laying your heart bare for everyone; it's about choosing to be real with the people who matter, the ones who've earned a place in your life.

Vulnerability is the doorway to intimacy. It's what allows two people to see each other for who they truly are, beyond the facades and expectations. When you let yourself be vulnerable, you're saying, *I trust you with this part of me.* And in doing so, you invite the other person to do the same. This exchange of openness builds a connection that's genuine, a bond that isn't based on appearances but on understanding and acceptance. Vulnerability creates a safe space where both people can show up fully, without the fear of judgment, knowing they're accepted as they are.

One of the first steps in practicing vulnerability is letting go of the need to appear perfect. Perfectionism is a shield that keeps people at a distance. When you're constantly trying to present an idealized version of yourself, you're not allowing others to truly see you, and you're not giving yourself permission to be human. Instead, allow yourself to show up as you are, flaws and all. Share your struggles, your uncertainties, and your growth. People don't connect with perfection; they connect with realness. The more authentic you are, the more meaningful your connections become.

To cultivate vulnerability, start by sharing small things. You don't have to jump straight into deep conversations about your past or your biggest fears. Begin with the day-to-day moments, like expressing how you feel about something important or sharing a personal goal. Small acts of openness build trust, creating a foundation for deeper vulnerability. As you get comfortable with sharing, you'll find it easier to open up about bigger things. Vulnerability is a gradual process, a series of small steps that create a relationship where both people feel safe to be themselves.

Another essential part of vulnerability is learning to communicate your needs. Often, we hold back from expressing our needs out of fear that we'll be seen as too much, too needy, or too dependent. But true connection requires honesty, and that includes being honest about what you need in a relationship. Whether it's emotional support, quality time, or just someone to listen, sharing your needs allows the other person to understand and support you more fully. When both people feel free to express their needs, the relationship becomes a place of mutual support and understanding, a space where both are empowered to give and receive.

Practicing vulnerability also means being open about your boundaries. Vulnerability isn't about letting people into every part of your life; it's about inviting them into the spaces where connection feels genuine. Boundaries allow you to share yourself in a way that feels safe and authentic. Let the people in your life know what you're comfortable sharing, what you need space for, and where your limits are. Vulnerability and boundaries work hand-in-hand; they allow you to be open without losing your sense of self. Healthy vulnerability is about choosing how much to share, based on trust and respect.

One of the challenges of vulnerability is the fear of rejection. Opening up to someone means there's a chance they might not understand, or worse, that they might judge. But here's the thing: rejection isn't a reflection of your worth; it's simply an indication that this person may not be able to hold space for you. Not everyone will be ready or willing to connect on a deeper level, and that's okay. Vulnerability helps you filter out relationships that aren't right for you. It allows you to focus on building connections with people who respect your openness, who value your honesty, and who are willing to be vulnerable with you in return.

Embracing vulnerability also involves practicing forgiveness, both for yourself and others. Sometimes, people will make mistakes in relationships. They may unintentionally hurt you or struggle to meet your needs. Vulnerability means being willing to have difficult conversations, to communicate openly, and to offer grace when things don't go perfectly. It means allowing room for growth, for apologies, and for healing. Vulnerability is about being open to the imperfections of others and accepting that relationships are a work in progress, a journey of growth and learning.

Ultimately, vulnerability is about choosing to show up as your true self. It's about building relationships that don't require you to hide, shrink, or pretend. When you embrace vulnerability, you're choosing connections that are meaningful, relationships where both people feel valued, understood, and supported. Vulnerability is what turns acquaintances into friends, friends into family, and family into a source of deep, unconditional love.

Because here's the truth: vulnerability isn't weakness; it's strength. It's the courage to be real in a world that often values appearances. And when you allow yourself to be vulnerable, you're choosing to live a life that's rich in connection, a life where love isn't just an idea but a real, tangible experience, rooted in openness, acceptance, and the freedom to be yourself.

# Chapter 15:
# Embracing Change and Growth

Change is the engine of growth. Without change, we stay the same, stuck in the same patterns, the same routines, and the same mindset. But as natural as change is, it can be intimidating, even scary. The unknown is uncomfortable because it demands that we leave behind the familiar and venture into new territory. And yet, if you're committed to growth, change is something you must embrace. It's the doorway to new experiences, insights, and opportunities. When you let go of the fear of change, you open yourself to the life you're meant to live—a life that's dynamic, evolving, and full of possibility.

The fear of change often comes from the stories we tell ourselves about the unknown. We imagine worst-case scenarios, or we assume that because we don't know what's coming, it must be bad. But here's the truth: not all change is negative. In fact, many of the most positive experiences in life come from unexpected changes. The unknown can be a place of excitement, adventure, and growth, if you're willing to approach it with an open mind. Instead of seeing change as something to fear, try seeing it as an opportunity to explore, to learn, and to evolve.

One of the first steps in embracing change is reframing uncertainty as potential. Instead of asking, *What if something goes wrong?* try asking, *What if this leads to something amazing?* Change doesn't guarantee hardship; it simply opens the door to different possibilities. Each time you face change, remind yourself that there's also a chance for something beautiful, something transformative. Embracing uncertainty as potential allows you to look at change not as a threat but as an invitation to experience life more fully.

A practical approach to easing the fear of change is to take small steps outside your comfort zone. You don't have to make a huge, life-altering decision right away; start with small changes that stretch you just a bit. Try a new activity, meet new people, or approach a familiar problem from a new perspective. Each small step builds your resilience, making bigger changes feel less overwhelming. By gradually expanding your comfort zone, you're showing yourself that you're capable of handling the unknown, that you can navigate change without losing your balance.

Another powerful way to embrace change is to reflect on past experiences where change led to growth. Think about times when you faced a difficult or uncertain situation and ended up stronger or wiser because of it. Often, the hardest changes lead to the most meaningful transformations. By reminding yourself of the growth you've experienced in the past, you're reinforcing your ability to handle whatever comes next. You've faced change before, and you're still here, still growing. This perspective gives you the confidence to face future changes with courage and resilience.

When approaching change, it's also important to stay grounded in your values. Change can feel destabilizing, but your values act as an anchor, a reminder of what truly matters to you. When you're clear on your values, you're able to approach change with a sense of purpose and direction. Instead of letting fear dictate your actions, you're guided by what aligns with who you are. Your values provide stability, allowing you to adapt to change while staying true to yourself. No matter how much life shifts, you have a foundation that keeps you grounded.

One helpful practice for embracing change is visualization. Picture yourself moving through the change you're facing, adapting, and finding your way. Imagine yourself thriving in the new situation, feeling strong, capable, and at peace. Visualization isn't about pretending change is easy; it's about building mental resilience, showing yourself that you're capable of handling new experiences. By seeing yourself navigating change successfully, you're conditioning your mind to respond with confidence rather than fear. This mental rehearsal prepares you to face the unknown with a sense of calm and trust.

Lastly, embracing change means letting go of the need for total control. Growth happens when you allow life to unfold, when you stop trying to predict every outcome and trust that you'll handle whatever comes. Trying to control change only creates stress and anxiety, a sense that you're always on edge. But when you release the need for control, you're giving yourself permission to relax, to be present, and to experience life as it is. Trust yourself to adapt, to learn, and to find joy in the unexpected. The unknown doesn't need to be feared; it can be an invitation to a life that's richer, more dynamic, and more aligned with your growth.

Because here's the truth: change is part of life, and growth is about learning to flow with it, not resist it. When you embrace the unknown, you're opening yourself to a life that's full of discovery, a life where each new chapter brings something meaningful. By letting go of fear and choosing curiosity, you're giving yourself permission to live fully, to grow, and to create a life that's not limited by the familiar but expanded by possibility.

Growth isn't a constant upward trajectory; it's a rhythm, a series of seasons. Sometimes, you're in a season of expansion, where everything feels fresh, and you're motivated to pursue new goals, connect with new people, or dive into new projects. Other times, you're in a season of stillness, where growth feels slower, where you're reflecting, resting, or even facing challenges that force you to pause. But here's the truth: both seasons are necessary. Just as nature has cycles of growth and dormancy, so do we. Embracing the ebb and flow of life's seasons allows you to honor each phase without judgment, without feeling like you constantly need to be achieving.

In a world that often glorifies productivity and busyness, it's easy to feel like you should always be moving forward. But growth isn't just about doing; it's also about being. Some of the most profound growth happens in seasons of rest, in times when you're not actively "doing" but are simply allowing yourself to recharge, reflect, and realign. These periods are not setbacks or failures—they're a chance to reconnect with yourself, to process what you've been through, and to prepare for the next season of expansion. By embracing the quieter seasons, you're acknowledging that growth isn't a race; it's a journey that respects your pace and your needs.

One way to honor life's seasons is to practice self-awareness. Pay attention to the rhythms of your own energy, motivation, and focus. Notice when you're feeling inspired and driven, and also notice when you're feeling the need to slow down or step back. Self-awareness allows you to recognize what season you're in and to respond accordingly. If you're in a period of rest, give yourself permission to step away from the pressure to constantly produce. If you're in a period of growth, embrace the momentum and pursue your goals. This awareness helps you make choices that respect where you are, rather than forcing yourself into a season that doesn't align.

Another key to adapting to life's seasons is learning to set boundaries with yourself and others. When you're in a quieter season, it's easy to feel guilty for not being as active or social as usual. But setting boundaries around your energy protects your well-being and allows you to honor your current season without apology. Communicate your needs to those around you, letting them know if you need space, time, or understanding. Boundaries aren't about isolating yourself; they're about creating an environment where you can recharge and refocus, preparing yourself for the seasons of growth that lie ahead.

To embrace life's natural ebb and flow, practice acceptance rather than resistance. Resisting a season—whether it's one of growth or rest—only creates stress. If you're constantly wishing you were somewhere else, you're missing out on the lessons that each phase has to offer. Accept where you are, trust that this season has a purpose, and remind yourself that no season lasts forever. Each phase of life brings insights and growth, even if it's not obvious at the time. Acceptance allows you to live fully in each season, making the most of the opportunities and challenges that come with it.

Reflecting on your journey can also help you appreciate life's seasons. Look back on times when you faced challenges or slowed down and see how they contributed to your growth. Often, the insights we gain in quieter periods provide the foundation for future achievements. Reflection helps you see that each season has value, that even the slower or more difficult phases played a part in making you who you are today. When you recognize the wisdom that comes from each season, you're more likely to approach future phases with gratitude and openness rather than frustration.

Finally, remember that growth is cyclical, not linear. Just because you've grown through something once doesn't mean you'll never revisit it. Life has a way of bringing us back to certain lessons, showing us new depths each time. This isn't regression; it's a chance to deepen your understanding, to approach familiar challenges with new perspectives. Growth loops back on itself, allowing you to refine, reassess, and integrate your experiences more fully. Embracing this cyclical nature helps you approach life with patience, knowing that each season brings something new, even if it looks familiar.

By honoring life's seasons, you're allowing yourself to grow in a way that's natural, sustainable, and true to who you are. You're no longer forcing progress but instead aligning with the flow of your own journey. Some seasons will be full of action and excitement, while others will be quiet, introspective, or even challenging. But each season holds value, each phase is part of your growth, and each moment is bringing you closer to the person you're meant to become.

Because here's the truth: growth isn't about constant upward motion; it's about embracing the ebb and flow, the stillness and the movement, the highs and the lows. And when you allow yourself to move with life's seasons, you're choosing a path that respects your rhythm, honors your needs, and brings a sense of peace that only comes from truly embracing the journey.

Growth doesn't happen without discomfort. We'd all love for change to be easy, for growth to feel like a smooth journey, but the reality is that true transformation often requires moving through pain, fear, and discomfort. Discomfort is a signal that you're stepping outside your comfort zone, that you're pushing beyond the familiar. It's a sign of progress, not failure. When you embrace discomfort, you're choosing strength, resilience, and the courage to grow through even the hardest moments.

Discomfort isn't something to be feared; it's something to be understood. When you feel uncomfortable, take a moment to check in with yourself. Ask yourself, *What is this feeling trying to tell me?* Sometimes, discomfort is a reminder that you're pushing your limits in a healthy way, challenging beliefs or habits that no longer serve you. Other times, it can indicate areas where you need to grow, skills you need to develop, or boundaries you need to set. Discomfort is a teacher, showing you where growth is possible, where old patterns can be replaced with new ones. Embracing it with curiosity allows you to see it as part of your journey, rather than something to avoid.

One way to build resilience in uncomfortable situations is to practice grounding techniques. When you're feeling overwhelmed, bring yourself back to the present moment. Take deep breaths, focus on your surroundings, or engage in an activity that centers you. Grounding yourself reminds you that discomfort is temporary, that it's a wave you can ride rather than a force that will overwhelm you. Each time you ground yourself, you're building your capacity to handle discomfort without being controlled by it. This practice teaches you to stay steady, even when emotions feel intense, allowing you to approach challenges from a place of calm.

Another powerful tool for embracing discomfort is self-compassion. When we're facing challenges, our inner critic often speaks up, telling us that we're not doing enough, that we're failing, or that we should be handling things better. But self-compassion shifts the focus from criticism to kindness. Remind yourself that growth is hard, that you're allowed to struggle, and that discomfort doesn't mean you're failing. It means you're moving forward. Speak to yourself as you would to a friend, offering words of encouragement and understanding. Self-compassion turns discomfort into an opportunity for self-care, helping you build resilience from a place of gentleness rather than judgment.

A practical exercise for working through discomfort is to create a "discomfort journal." Each time you face a challenging moment, write down what you're feeling, what thoughts are coming up, and what actions you took. Over time, you'll start to see patterns—how you react to discomfort, what strategies help, and where your strengths lie. This journal becomes a record of your resilience, a reminder that you've faced difficult moments before and made it through. Seeing your own growth in writing can be a powerful motivator, especially in moments when you're tempted to give up.

Setting small, achievable goals within uncomfortable situations can also help you embrace discomfort more fully. Sometimes, the hardest part of growth is feeling like the journey is too overwhelming. Break it down. Instead of focusing on the entire challenge, set a small goal you can accomplish right now. Each small step reinforces that you're capable, that you can handle the discomfort without being consumed by it. Over time, these small actions build your confidence, showing you that discomfort is manageable, that each step brings you closer to the other side of the challenge.

Lastly, embracing discomfort means letting go of the need for immediate results. Growth takes time, and discomfort is often the sign that you're in the thick of it. Resist the urge to look for instant solutions or to "fix" everything right away. Instead, focus on progress, no matter how small it may seem. Trust that the discomfort is part of the process and that it will eventually lead to change, even if the results aren't immediately visible. Patience helps you accept discomfort as a temporary state, reminding you that each moment of unease is bringing you closer to the growth you're working toward.

Embracing discomfort is about choosing courage over comfort, choosing growth over stagnation. It's about accepting that the most meaningful changes often come from the hardest moments. Discomfort may feel overwhelming at times, but it's also a reminder of your resilience, your strength, and your willingness to evolve. When you learn to sit with discomfort rather than run from it, you're opening yourself up to a life that's richer, a journey that's more fulfilling, and a version of yourself that's stronger than you ever imagined.

Because here's the truth: growth isn't supposed to be easy; it's supposed to be transformative. And when you embrace the discomfort, you're choosing a life that's dynamic, courageous, and true to who you are becoming.

Growth doesn't just require change; it requires resilience—the inner strength to keep going, to adapt, and to rise even after life knocks you down. Resilience is what lets you take the lessons from every challenge, what allows you to transform hardships into strengths, and what gives you the courage to keep moving forward, no matter how difficult the journey becomes. Building resilience isn't about never feeling pain or avoiding failure; it's about learning to navigate both with grace, courage, and the understanding that each setback is part of a much bigger picture.

Resilience starts with mindset. It's about choosing to see challenges not as threats but as opportunities for growth. This doesn't mean downplaying pain or pretending everything is fine; it means accepting that life will have its ups and downs and that you are capable of handling them. When you choose to view obstacles as chances to grow, you're empowering yourself to approach challenges with curiosity rather than fear. You're shifting from a victim mindset to one of strength, seeing each hardship as something that, while difficult, can also shape you in meaningful ways.

One powerful way to build resilience is through gratitude. This might seem counterintuitive, especially in difficult times, but gratitude shifts your focus from what's going wrong to what's still good, stable, or positive in your life. Gratitude doesn't erase challenges, but it reminds you that even in the hardest moments, there's something worth holding onto. Each time you find something to appreciate, you're reinforcing the strength within you. Gratitude builds resilience by grounding you in the present, by giving you a foundation of positivity to lean on, and by reminding you that life isn't defined by its hardships alone.

Practicing adaptability is also essential to resilience. Life rarely goes according to plan, and being able to pivot, to adjust, and to stay open to new paths is a critical part of lasting growth. Adaptability doesn't mean you have to let go of your goals or dreams; it means you're willing to find alternative ways to reach them. When something doesn't work out, ask yourself, *What can I try instead?* or *What's another way to approach this?* This flexibility helps you keep moving forward, even when the original path isn't available. Adaptability reminds you that setbacks aren't dead ends; they're simply detours that bring new perspectives and sometimes even better opportunities.

Another way to build resilience is by nurturing your support network. Resilience isn't about going it alone; it's about knowing when to lean on others. Surround yourself with people who believe in you, who remind you of your strength, and who are there to lift you up when things get tough. Whether it's friends, family, mentors, or a support group, having people who understand and support you creates a safety net. It's a reminder that you're not facing challenges in isolation and that others have faced similar battles and come out stronger. Connection builds resilience by reminding you that growth doesn't have to be a solo journey.

Self-care is also a fundamental part of resilience. You can't face challenges if you're constantly running on empty. Taking care of your physical, emotional, and mental well-being gives you the stamina to keep going, even when things are difficult. Self-care isn't indulgence; it's preparation. It's ensuring that you're in a strong place to tackle life's challenges. Whether it's exercise, meditation, creative hobbies, or simply getting enough rest, self-care builds resilience by keeping you grounded, focused, and prepared to face whatever comes your way.

Reflecting on past successes and challenges also strengthens resilience. Look back on times when you faced difficulties and remember how you overcame them. Reflect on the qualities that got you through—courage, persistence, resourcefulness—and recognize that those qualities are still within you. By acknowledging your past resilience, you're reminding yourself that you have the tools, the experience, and the strength to handle future challenges. Each hardship you've overcome has prepared you for the next, giving you a reserve of strength that grows with every obstacle you face.

Resilience is a skill that you build over time, one that becomes a source of unwavering strength. It doesn't mean you won't face setbacks, that you won't feel pain or disappointment. It means that you're able to stand back up, that you're willing to keep going, and that you have faith in your ability to find meaning, even in hardship. Resilience doesn't remove the difficulties from your path; it transforms how you approach them, turning each challenge into a stepping stone, each setback into a lesson, and each hardship into an opportunity for growth.

Because here's the truth: resilience is the foundation of lasting growth. It's the courage to keep showing up, the strength to keep moving forward, and the belief that no matter what happens, you're capable of handling it. And when you build resilience, you're choosing a life where growth isn't dependent on circumstances but on your own inner strength—a life where each moment, each experience, brings you closer to the person you're meant to become.

# Chapter 16: Living Authentically

Living authentically is one of the most liberating things you can do for yourself. It means showing up as you are, without filtering, without pretending, and without trying to fit into someone else's mold. Authenticity is about aligning your words, actions, and choices with your true self. It's about being unapologetically you, even if it means standing out, being misunderstood, or challenging others' expectations. When you live authentically, you're no longer compromising who you are to fit in or be accepted. Instead, you're choosing a life that feels real, a life that's yours in every sense.

Authenticity starts with self-awareness. To live authentically, you need to know who you are—what you believe in, what you value, and what you want out of life. This requires being honest with yourself, reflecting on your motivations, and tuning into what truly matters to you. Self-awareness allows you to make choices that honor your values rather than those of society or others. It's about knowing your strengths, acknowledging your flaws, and embracing every part of who you are. When you're grounded in self-awareness, authenticity becomes a natural extension of your inner truth.

One of the biggest obstacles to authenticity is the fear of judgment. We often hold back from expressing ourselves fully because we're afraid of what others might think. But here's the reality: people will judge you no matter what you do. If you're constantly editing yourself to avoid judgment, you'll never experience the freedom of living as your true self. Authenticity means releasing the need for approval and choosing to show up as you are, even if it means some people won't understand. By letting go of this fear, you're creating space for people who genuinely appreciate you to enter your life.

Another key to authenticity is setting boundaries around your energy. When you're authentic, you're more selective about the situations and relationships you engage in. You're no longer sacrificing your peace or pretending to be someone else to make others comfortable. Setting boundaries means choosing to surround yourself with people who respect and support the real you, not just the version that's convenient for them. Boundaries allow you to protect your energy, to honor your values, and to live in a way that's aligned with who you truly are.

Practicing honesty is essential to authenticity. This doesn't mean being brutally honest or sharing every thought without filter; it means being truthful with yourself and others about what you want, what you need, and what you believe. Honesty helps you create relationships based on trust, not pretense. It allows others to see the real you and invites them to do the same. When you're honest about who you are, you're building connections that are based on respect and understanding rather than appearances. Honesty brings depth to your relationships, creating bonds that are genuine, fulfilling, and rooted in acceptance.

Living authentically also requires self-acceptance. You can't be real with others if you're still hiding from yourself. Self-acceptance means embracing all parts of you—the strengths, the quirks, and even the imperfections. It's understanding that you don't have to be perfect to be worthy, that your flaws don't diminish your value. Self-acceptance is the foundation of authenticity because it allows you to show up without fear, knowing that you're enough just as you are. When you accept yourself, you're no longer looking for others to validate you, freeing you to live without apology.

A practical exercise for authenticity is to create a "values list." Write down the things that truly matter to you—the principles, beliefs, and passions that define who you are. This list serves as a guide, reminding you of your core self when life gets overwhelming or when you're tempted to compromise for acceptance. Each time you make a choice, reflect on whether it aligns with these values. This practice helps you stay true to yourself, ensuring that your life reflects what's meaningful to you rather than what's expected by others.

Lastly, living authentically means letting go of the need to please everyone. People-pleasing often comes from a desire to avoid conflict, to be liked, or to keep the peace. But constantly pleasing others means neglecting your own needs, silencing your own voice, and sacrificing your own happiness. Authenticity requires choosing self-respect over approval, choosing to be real over being agreeable. It's about knowing that the right people will respect your authenticity, and that those who don't aren't meant to be part of your journey. Letting go of people-pleasing frees you to live a life that's true, a life that belongs to you.

Living authentically is a choice—a choice to honor your truth, to respect your journey, and to live without apology. It's about creating a life that resonates with who you are, not who others want you to be. And when you live authentically, you're not just building a life that feels right; you're also creating space for real connections, for meaningful experiences, and for a sense of freedom that can only come from living as your true self.

Because here's the truth: authenticity isn't just about being yourself; it's about loving yourself enough to live without filters, without compromises, and without regret. And when you make that choice, you're choosing a life that's yours, a life that's honest, and a life that's truly worth living.

One of the most empowering aspects of living authentically is the freedom to stand firm in your beliefs. In a world that often pressures us to conform, staying true to what you believe in is an act of courage. It's a choice to honor your truth, to live by your own standards, and to stay aligned with your values even when others disagree. Owning your beliefs without needing validation means you're no longer swayed by outside opinions or approval. You're free to live in a way that feels right to you, rather than constantly adjusting to fit someone else's expectations.

Standing firm in your beliefs requires self-confidence. Confidence isn't about being loud or trying to convince others that you're right; it's about feeling secure enough in yourself that you don't need validation. When you're confident in your beliefs, you're less affected by criticism or judgment. This confidence doesn't come from always being right—it comes from knowing you've thought deeply about your values and that they align with who you are. True confidence allows you to stand your ground without needing others to agree with you. It's a quiet strength that comes from within, rooted in authenticity.

One of the most powerful steps to standing firm in your beliefs is learning to say "no" when something doesn't align with your values. Sometimes, it's tempting to go along with others just to keep the peace or to avoid conflict. But each time you compromise your values, you're chipping away at your authenticity. Saying "no" to situations, behaviors, or conversations that go against your beliefs is an act of self-respect. It's a way of saying, *I value my truth enough to protect it.* Over time, saying "no" becomes easier, and each choice reinforces your commitment to living authentically.

Another way to strengthen your resolve is to educate yourself about your beliefs. When you know why you believe what you do, you're better prepared to stand firm in it. This doesn't mean you need to have every answer or be able to debate every point; it simply means you've taken the time to understand your beliefs on a personal level. Whether it's a social issue, a personal value, or a spiritual belief, learning more about it reinforces your confidence. Knowledge helps you articulate your beliefs with clarity, allowing you to express your truth in a way that feels grounded and authentic.

Surrounding yourself with like-minded people is also essential. It's easier to stay true to your beliefs when you're around people who share similar values or, at the very least, respect your values. This doesn't mean isolating yourself from others who think differently, but it does mean prioritizing relationships that support your authenticity. When you have a strong network of people who uplift and respect you, you're more resilient against external pressures. These connections remind you that you're not alone, that there are others who see and appreciate you for who you are.

Standing firm in your beliefs also involves letting go of the need to defend them constantly. Not everyone will understand or agree with your values, and that's okay. Authenticity isn't about proving yourself to others; it's about being true to yourself. If someone challenges your beliefs, respond calmly and respectfully, but don't feel obligated to argue or justify yourself. Remember, the people who genuinely respect you won't demand explanations or try to change your mind. They'll respect you for your authenticity, even if they don't share your perspective.

A helpful practice for strengthening your authenticity is daily affirmation. Each morning, remind yourself of your values and why they're important to you. Affirm that you have the strength to stand by them, regardless of others' opinions. Simple affirmations like *I am true to myself* or *My values guide me, not the approval of others* reinforce your commitment to authenticity. Over time, these affirmations become part of your mindset, a reminder that you're capable of living your truth without apology.

Lastly, give yourself grace as you navigate your path. Standing firm in your beliefs doesn't mean you'll never waver or question yourself. Self-doubt is natural, and moments of uncertainty are part of the journey. Authenticity isn't about being rigid; it's about honoring your journey, even when it feels challenging. Each time you question, reflect, or adjust, you're growing. You're not expected to be perfect, only to stay committed to living in a way that feels true to you.

Because here's the truth: owning your beliefs is about more than just being "right"; it's about being real. When you live by your truth, you're choosing to live fully, freely, and without apology. And each time you stand firm in your beliefs, you're creating a life that's grounded, meaningful, and deeply aligned with who you are.

Living authentically doesn't mean living perfectly. In fact, it's the opposite—it's about embracing your imperfections, allowing yourself to be fully human, and understanding that realness is far more valuable than any illusion of flawlessness. Authenticity isn't about having it all together; it's about showing up as you are, with all your quirks, mistakes, and contradictions. When you accept your imperfections, you're giving yourself permission to be real, to let go of the pressure to perform, and to live a life that's honest, unfiltered, and deeply fulfilling.

One of the first steps in embracing imperfection is changing how you talk to yourself. We're often our own harshest critics, quick to magnify our flaws and downplay our strengths. But self-criticism only pulls you further from authenticity, keeping you stuck in a loop of shame and self-doubt. Start by practicing self-compassion, speaking to yourself as you would to a friend. Instead of saying, *I'm not good enough,* try saying, *I'm doing my best, and that's enough.* Self-compassion helps you view your imperfections with kindness, allowing you to see them not as flaws but as parts of what make you uniquely you.

Another powerful way to embrace imperfection is to focus on progress, not perfection. Authenticity is a journey, not a destination, and growth happens gradually. You're not expected to have everything figured out, nor should you be. Embrace each step of your journey, each lesson learned, and each mistake made. When you focus on progress, you're celebrating your growth rather than constantly chasing an ideal that doesn't exist. Progress reminds you that each experience, no matter how imperfect, is a step closer to living more fully as yourself.

Letting go of comparisons is also essential to embracing imperfection. In today's world, we're constantly exposed to others' curated lives, which can make us feel inadequate. But comparing yourself to others only keeps you from appreciating your own journey. Remember, everyone has their own struggles, insecurities, and imperfections, even if they're not visible. Each time you find yourself comparing, shift your focus back to your own path, your own progress. Your journey doesn't need to look like anyone else's to be valuable. When you release the need to measure up to others, you're free to embrace your life on your own terms.

Authenticity also involves sharing your imperfections with others. Being open about your struggles, uncertainties, and mistakes is a powerful way to build real connections. Vulnerability invites others to see the real you, creating relationships that are based on acceptance rather than performance. When you're willing to show up as imperfect, you're giving others permission to do the same. This openness builds trust, allowing for connections that go beyond appearances. Embracing imperfection in relationships creates a space where both people can feel safe, supported, and accepted for who they truly are.

A helpful practice for embracing imperfection is to celebrate your uniqueness. Take time to recognize what makes you different—your quirks, your perspectives, and your way of seeing the world. These are the things that make you memorable, that bring color and depth to your life. Each time you celebrate your uniqueness, you're reinforcing that you don't have to conform or hide parts of yourself to be valuable. Authenticity isn't about fitting in; it's about standing out in a way that feels true to who you are. By embracing what makes you unique, you're affirming your right to live unapologetically.

Forgiving yourself is also key to living authentically. We all have moments we wish we could take back, choices we'd make differently if given the chance. But holding onto regret only keeps you tied to a past version of yourself. Self-forgiveness is an act of freedom, a way of letting go of the weight of past mistakes. When you forgive yourself, you're choosing to learn, to grow, and to move forward without carrying the burden of perfection. Forgiveness doesn't erase your mistakes, but it allows you to see them as part of your journey, as experiences that have shaped who you are today.

Finally, embracing imperfection means trusting that you are enough, as you are, in this moment. You don't need to wait until you're "better" to be worthy of love, happiness, or success. You are enough right now, with all your strengths and all your flaws. When you trust in your own worth, you're free to live authentically, to pursue your dreams without constantly second-guessing yourself. Trusting in your enoughness is the foundation of authenticity, allowing you to show up fully, to express yourself freely, and to live a life that's aligned with your truest self.

Because here's the truth: authenticity isn't about perfection; it's about presence. It's about being here, right now, with all your imperfections, and knowing that you are worthy of living a life that's real, a life that's yours. When you embrace your imperfections, you're choosing to live in a way that's honest, liberating, and deeply fulfilling. You're choosing a life that's true, a life that celebrates who you are rather than who you think you should be.

Living authentically isn't just about self-reflection or embracing imperfections; it's about actively creating a life that reflects your truest self. This means making choices that honor your values, building relationships that support your growth, and following a path that feels meaningful to you, not one dictated by others' expectations. When you align your actions, relationships, and daily life with who you are at your core, you're creating a life that feels whole, a life that's yours in every sense. Authenticity isn't just a mindset; it's a practice, one that's reflected in every choice you make.

Creating a life that's yours begins with aligning your actions with your values. Start by identifying what matters most to you—whether it's honesty, creativity, family, or personal freedom. These values act as your compass, guiding you in every decision, big or small. Ask yourself, *Is this choice aligned with my values? Does it reflect who I am or who I want to become?* When your actions align with your values, you're living with integrity, which creates a sense of inner peace. Each value-driven choice strengthens your authenticity, reinforcing that you're on a path that's true to you.

One of the most powerful ways to build an authentic life is to pursue passions that genuinely resonate with you. Too often, we feel pressured to follow paths that look "successful" to others or that fit societal standards of achievement. But authenticity is about creating success on your own terms, about following pursuits that bring you joy, curiosity, or fulfillment, even if they're unconventional. Whether it's a career, a hobby, or a creative project, choose what speaks to you. When you pursue what you're passionate about, you're living a life that's driven by purpose rather than by others' approval.

Aligning your relationships with your authentic self is also essential. The people you surround yourself with have a huge impact on your life, shaping your energy, mindset, and overall well-being. Building authentic relationships means choosing to connect with people who respect your values, who support your growth, and who encourage you to be yourself. It also means letting go of relationships that feel forced, judgmental, or draining. Authentic connections don't require you to pretend or change; they allow you to show up fully as you are. When you surround yourself with people who truly see you, you're creating a support network that nurtures your authenticity.

A practical way to align your life with authenticity is to simplify. When we're overwhelmed with commitments, obligations, or distractions, it's easy to lose touch with what matters. Simplifying your life—whether it's decluttering your environment, streamlining your routines, or cutting back on activities that drain you—creates space for what's truly meaningful. By focusing on what truly aligns with your values and goals, you're able to invest your time and energy in things that bring you fulfillment. Simplifying isn't about doing less; it's about doing more of what's aligned with your authentic self.

Embracing intentionality is also key to creating a life that's yours. Each day, make choices that bring you closer to the person you want to be. Whether it's how you spend your time, the goals you pursue, or the people you connect with, be intentional in aligning your actions with your vision of an authentic life. This intentionality turns ordinary moments into meaningful ones, reminding you that authenticity is built in the small, daily decisions. When you approach life with purpose, you're actively creating a life that's aligned, a life that feels real, fulfilling, and uniquely yours.

Living authentically also requires resilience, because choosing your own path isn't always easy. You'll likely face criticism, doubt, or pressure to conform, especially if your choices don't fit the usual mold. But resilience gives you the strength to stay true to yourself, even when it's challenging. Remind yourself that authenticity isn't about pleasing others; it's about honoring your truth. Resilience helps you navigate the ups and downs of living authentically, allowing you to stay committed to your journey despite external pressures. Each time you choose to stay true to yourself, you're reinforcing your commitment to a life that's yours.

Finally, creating a life that's yours means celebrating the journey, not just the destination. Authenticity isn't something you "achieve"; it's something you practice, something that evolves as you grow. Each choice, each moment of self-reflection, each time you show up as your true self—these are all parts of building an authentic life. Take time to celebrate your progress, to appreciate the small wins, and to acknowledge the courage it takes to live without compromise. Living authentically is a journey, one that brings you closer to a life that feels meaningful, whole, and aligned with who you truly are.

Because here's the truth: an authentic life isn't about fitting in; it's about standing out in a way that feels true. It's about creating a life that reflects your values, that celebrates your passions, and that supports your growth. When you live authentically, you're not just existing; you're thriving, living a life that's vibrant, fulfilling, and fully, unapologetically yours.

# Chapter 17: Finding Purpose

Purpose isn't just a word; it's a compass. It's what gives your life depth, meaning, and direction. Finding your "why" allows you to wake up each day with a sense of intention, knowing that your actions and choices are building toward something bigger. Purpose doesn't necessarily mean you have one singular, grand goal—it can be found in the small things, the daily acts that make life feel meaningful. Whether it's creating, helping others, building something lasting, or simply living fully, your purpose is what keeps you moving forward with passion, even when life is challenging.

To start defining your "why," take time to reflect on what genuinely moves you. Ask yourself, *What makes me feel alive? What am I naturally drawn to? What values do I hold closest?* Purpose is often found in the places where your passions, talents, and values intersect. It's not about choosing a life path that sounds impressive; it's about choosing one that feels meaningful to you. Purpose is personal, something that resonates with your core, regardless of what others might think. When you align with your "why," you're building a life that feels deeply authentic, driven by what matters most to you.

One way to clarify your purpose is to look at your past experiences. Think about times when you felt the most fulfilled or proud of yourself. These moments often hold clues to what gives your life meaning. Perhaps you felt a deep sense of purpose when you helped someone, created something unique, or overcame a personal challenge. By reflecting on these experiences, you'll start to see patterns—values or themes that repeat themselves. These patterns often reveal your purpose, showing you what gives you a sense of fulfillment, regardless of the circumstances.

It's also helpful to explore what frustrates or challenges you. Sometimes, purpose is found not just in what brings joy, but in what sparks a desire for change. If certain issues or causes make you feel passionate, angry, or determined, these feelings might be pointing you toward a purpose that involves addressing them. Purpose isn't always comfortable; it often involves standing up for something, improving something, or creating something better. By leaning into what challenges or frustrates you, you're tapping into a deeper level of purpose, one that pushes you to make a difference.

Purpose isn't static; it's something that evolves with you. Allow yourself the freedom to explore, experiment, and redefine your "why" as you grow. Your purpose today might look different from your purpose five or ten years from now, and that's okay. Purpose is a living part of who you are, shaped by your experiences, your growth, and your changing perspective. By staying open to this evolution, you're honoring your journey and allowing your purpose to grow with you. You're creating a life that reflects where you are now, rather than trying to hold onto an outdated idea of purpose.

Another powerful way to connect with your purpose is through service. Often, we find purpose not only in what we do for ourselves but in what we do for others. Service doesn't have to mean working in a specific field or taking on a certain role; it's about contributing something positive to the world around you. It's about using your strengths, passions, and experiences to make a difference, whether it's in your family, your community, or on a larger scale. Purpose through service connects you to something beyond yourself, giving you a sense of contribution, impact, and fulfillment.

Living with purpose also involves letting go of perfectionism. Purpose isn't about getting everything right or achieving flawless success. It's about showing up each day with intention, even if the steps are small or imperfect. Purpose is found in the effort, in the commitment to living in alignment with your "why," rather than in achieving a perfect outcome. When you let go of perfectionism, you're allowing yourself to embrace purpose with authenticity, understanding that growth, mistakes, and learning are all part of the journey. Purpose isn't about doing it all right; it's about doing what feels right.

Lastly, remind yourself that purpose isn't always about knowing exactly where you're going; sometimes, it's simply about moving in the right direction. Purpose gives your life a sense of direction, a sense of forward momentum, but it doesn't mean you need to have everything figured out. Each step you take with intention brings you closer to a life that feels meaningful, even if you're still figuring out the details. Purpose isn't a destination; it's a guiding light, something that inspires you to keep growing, keep learning, and keep showing up as your true self.

Because here's the truth: purpose isn't something you find outside yourself; it's something you uncover within. It's the quiet knowing of what feels right, of what makes life feel worth living. When you connect with your "why," you're choosing to live with intention, to create a life that feels meaningful, and to embrace each moment as part of a bigger journey. And that's what purpose is—an invitation to live fully, to love deeply, and to make each day count.

Passion is one of the most powerful guides to purpose. When you follow what excites you, you're not only doing something that brings joy; you're also connecting with a deeper sense of fulfillment, something that energizes and inspires you. Passion is often the spark that leads to purpose, showing you the activities, causes, or projects that resonate with who you are at your core. By tuning into your passions, you're finding a path that doesn't just feel good in the moment but brings lasting meaning to your life.

Finding purpose through passion starts with curiosity. Think about the things that make you feel alive, the moments when you lose track of time or feel a surge of excitement. These are often signs of activities that bring you closer to your purpose. Don't overthink it; purpose isn't always found in grand gestures or major life shifts. Sometimes, it's in the small, everyday moments when you feel most connected to yourself. Curiosity allows you to explore these moments without pressure, helping you discover what truly resonates with you.

Another way to tap into passion is to revisit your childhood interests. Often, the things we loved as children hold clues to our deepest passions—passions that may have been put aside as we grew up. Whether it was drawing, storytelling, building, or helping others, these early interests reveal what brought you joy before life became filled with obligations or expectations. By reconnecting with these interests, you're reminding yourself of a simpler, truer version of what brings you joy. Reclaiming these forgotten passions is a way of finding purpose that's authentic, rooted in who you are at your core.

Purpose through passion doesn't mean you have to turn your passion into a career or make it your entire life. Sometimes, the pressure to "monetize" or "prove" our passions kills the very joy that makes them meaningful. Purpose can be found in simply making space for your passions, whether it's in the form of a hobby, a side project, or a weekend ritual. When you pursue passion without attaching expectations to it, you're free to explore, to grow, and to find purpose on your own terms. Purpose isn't about impressing others; it's about doing what makes you feel fulfilled.

If you're struggling to identify your passions, try experimenting. Sometimes, the only way to discover what excites you is to try new things, even if they're outside your comfort zone. Join a workshop, take up a new hobby, or volunteer for a cause that piques your interest. Each experience brings insight into what does or doesn't resonate with you, helping you refine your understanding of what brings you fulfillment. Experimenting opens you to a world of possibilities, allowing you to pursue purpose from a place of curiosity and openness.

A practical exercise to explore purpose through passion is the "Passion Map." Take a piece of paper and write down activities, causes, or ideas that interest you, no matter how big or small. Then, start drawing connections between these items.

You may find that certain themes emerge—helping others, creating, exploring nature, or learning new things. This map serves as a visual guide, showing you where your interests intersect and pointing you toward areas that might hold a deeper sense of purpose. Use this map as a reminder of what excites you and as a guide to help you pursue these interests intentionally.

Following passion also means letting go of the need for perfection. Too often, we abandon passions because we're afraid we won't be "good enough" or that others won't appreciate what we're doing. But purpose through passion isn't about mastery; it's about joy. You don't need to be the best artist, writer, speaker, or musician to find meaning in these pursuits. By letting go of the pressure to be perfect, you're freeing yourself to enjoy the process. Purpose isn't about achievement; it's about engaging fully in what makes you feel alive, without judgment or expectations.

Lastly, remember that passion often grows over time. You may not feel a deep sense of purpose right away, but as you invest in your passions, they become more meaningful. Each time you show up for what excites you, you're building a deeper connection to that passion. Purpose isn't always a sudden revelation; sometimes, it's a gradual unfolding, a deepening of interest that leads to fulfillment. By nurturing your passions consistently, you're allowing them to become an integral part of your life, one that brings purpose and joy.

Because here's the truth: purpose through passion is about living in a way that feels vibrant, engaged, and meaningful. It's about following what lights you up, even if the path isn't always clear. When you pursue your passions, you're choosing to live fully, to explore what makes you unique, and to build a life that's driven by joy, curiosity, and a sense of inner purpose. And that's what makes a life worth living—a life that's not just busy, but truly fulfilling.

Finding purpose isn't only about pursuing what excites you; it's also about finding ways to make an impact. When you contribute to something beyond yourself, whether it's helping others, championing a cause, or improving your community, you're connecting with a deeper sense of fulfillment. Purpose gains strength when it's tied to impact, when your actions not only bring you joy but also create a positive change in the world around you. Living with purpose means leaving a mark, however big or small, that makes a difference.

Aligning purpose with impact begins by asking yourself a simple question: *How can I use my strengths to help others?* Purpose doesn't require grand gestures or massive sacrifices. Sometimes, it's as simple as offering a listening ear, sharing knowledge, or creating something that brings value to others. Impact can be found in small acts of kindness, in conversations that inspire, or in contributions that uplift those around you. Purpose through impact is about using what you already have—your skills, your experiences, your passions—in ways that resonate with the needs of others.

To align purpose with impact, start by identifying causes that matter to you. Think about the issues or challenges that make you feel passionate, angry, or inspired to take action. These reactions often point to causes that align with your values and purpose. Whether it's environmental issues, social justice, mental health, or education, connecting with a cause gives your purpose a clear direction. Impact-driven purpose doesn't mean you have to dedicate your whole life to one issue; it's about channeling your energy toward something meaningful, knowing that your contributions, however small, make a difference.

Another powerful way to make an impact is to share your story. Every experience, every challenge, and every victory you've faced has shaped who you are—and sharing these stories can inspire, uplift, and motivate others. Sometimes, the impact we make comes from showing others that they're not alone, that growth and healing are possible. Your story has the power to impact those who might be struggling, offering hope, connection, and a reminder of resilience. By being open about your journey, you're contributing to a world where others feel seen, understood, and empowered.

Aligning purpose with impact also means building connections. When you align with others who share similar goals or values, your purpose becomes part of something bigger. These connections allow you to contribute on a larger scale, to collaborate, and to amplify your efforts. Join groups, organizations, or communities that are aligned with your cause. Surround yourself with people who inspire you, who remind you why your impact matters, and who share the drive to make a difference. Together, your collective efforts create a ripple effect, spreading purpose and positivity far beyond what you could do alone.

Impact-driven purpose also requires patience and consistency. Change doesn't happen overnight, and sometimes, the work of making a difference feels slow or challenging. But purpose isn't about instant results; it's about committing to the long-term vision, trusting that each small step contributes to a bigger picture. Whether you're volunteering, advocating, or simply showing up with integrity each day, your consistent efforts build momentum. Patience allows you to see the value in each action, even if the impact isn't immediately visible. Purpose isn't measured by speed; it's measured by dedication.

One practical exercise for aligning purpose with impact is to set "impact goals." These goals don't have to be huge; they could be as simple as reaching out to someone in need, raising awareness for a cause, or creating something that brings value to others. By setting small, achievable goals, you're actively making a difference without overwhelming yourself. Each goal achieved reinforces your purpose, reminding you that impact doesn't require perfection or grand gestures—it requires intention and follow-through.

Living with impact-driven purpose also means being open to change. Sometimes, as you engage with a cause or explore new ways of making a difference, your purpose may evolve. You may find yourself drawn to new causes, new roles, or new ways of contributing. Purpose is a journey, one that deepens as you grow and expand. By staying open to new experiences and perspectives, you're allowing your purpose to adapt, to become richer, and to reflect the person you're becoming.

Ultimately, aligning purpose with impact transforms the way you experience life. It gives you a reason to wake up each day with intention, knowing that your actions aren't just about personal success but about contributing to a greater good. Impact-driven purpose fills your life with meaning, connecting your efforts to something bigger than yourself. It reminds you that your life, your work, and your passions have the power to create a positive difference—a difference that resonates, even in the smallest ways.

Because here's the truth: purpose isn't just about what you do; it's about the impact you leave behind. When you live with impact-driven purpose, you're choosing to make your life matter, to leave the world a little better than you found it. And that's where true fulfillment lies—in knowing that your journey is creating a legacy, one that's built on purpose, passion, and the desire to make a meaningful impact.

Finding your purpose is a powerful beginning, but staying committed to it is where the real work lies. Purpose isn't always easy or straightforward. There will be setbacks, challenges, moments of self-doubt, and times when the path feels unclear. Staying committed to your purpose means holding onto your "why" even when things get tough. It's about resilience, about showing up each day with the determination to keep moving forward, and about believing in the value of your journey, regardless of external results.

One of the most important aspects of staying committed to your purpose is reconnecting with your "why." Purpose loses its power when it becomes just another task or obligation, so make time to reflect on what inspired you in the first place. Remind yourself of the values, passions, or causes that motivated you to pursue this path. Revisit your purpose statement, your passion map, or your impact goals. Regularly reconnecting with your "why" brings clarity and motivation, especially during times when your energy is low or the challenges seem overwhelming. It reminds you that your purpose is more than a to-do list—it's a calling.

To maintain focus, build small, purposeful rituals into your routine. These don't have to be complicated; even five minutes of daily reflection, journaling, or setting an intention for the day can reinforce your commitment. Purpose-driven rituals ground you, helping you center yourself in what truly matters. They act as reminders that each day is a chance to live with intention, to make small steps toward fulfilling your purpose. Over time, these rituals create a foundation of consistency, a way to stay connected to your purpose even on days when the bigger picture feels distant or daunting.

Another key to staying committed is setting flexible goals. Purpose isn't a straight line; it's a journey with twists, turns, and unexpected detours. Setting rigid goals can lead to frustration, especially when things don't go as planned. Instead, focus on setting goals that allow room for adaptation. These goals are grounded in your purpose but give you the flexibility to change direction if needed. When you allow your goals to evolve, you're honoring the dynamic nature of purpose, recognizing that growth often requires a willingness to pivot, learn, and try new approaches.

Resilience is also built by accepting the natural ebb and flow of motivation. There will be days when you feel deeply connected to your purpose, energized and inspired. But there will also be days when motivation wanes, when self-doubt creeps in, or when setbacks make you question your path. Accepting these fluctuations as part of the journey helps you stay committed without being discouraged by temporary setbacks. On low-motivation days, remind yourself that purpose isn't about constant inspiration; it's about commitment. Take a break if needed, recharge, and trust that your motivation will return.

A practical way to reinforce resilience is to celebrate small victories. Often, we're so focused on the end goal that we overlook the progress we're making along the way. Take time to acknowledge your achievements, no matter how small they may seem. Each step forward, each lesson learned, and each act of perseverance is a victory in itself. Celebrating these moments reinforces your commitment, reminding you that purpose is found not just in the destination but in the journey itself. Each small victory builds momentum, strengthening your resolve to keep going.

Surrounding yourself with supportive people also strengthens your commitment to purpose. Share your goals with people who understand and encourage you, who believe in your vision, and who remind you of your resilience when times are tough. Purpose-driven communities, whether it's friends, mentors, or online groups, provide a sense of accountability and motivation. These connections remind you that you're not alone on this journey, that others are walking similar paths, and that support is always available. The right people uplift you, helping you stay committed when your own strength wavers.

Lastly, staying committed to your purpose means giving yourself permission to grow and change. Purpose isn't always a fixed destination; it can evolve as you do. Allow yourself the freedom to explore new aspects of your purpose, to take on new challenges, and to let go of things that no longer serve your journey. Commitment doesn't mean being rigid; it means being open to growth, to redefining your purpose as you gain new insights and experiences. This flexibility allows your purpose to stay alive, relevant, and aligned with the person you're becoming.

Because here's the truth: purpose isn't a one-time decision; it's a daily choice. Staying committed means showing up, even when it's hard, even when the road is uncertain. It's about trusting that each step you take, each lesson you learn, and each moment of resilience is building a life that's meaningful, impactful, and uniquely yours. And when you stay committed to your purpose, you're not just living—you're creating a legacy, a life that's deeply fulfilling, and a journey that's truly worth every challenge.

# Chapter 18:
# Choosing Joy

Joy isn't just an emotion; it's a choice. While happiness can be fleeting, dependent on external circumstances or temporary pleasures, joy is deeper, rooted in a sense of inner contentment and fulfillment. Joy comes from within—it's something you cultivate regardless of what's happening around you. Choosing joy means finding reasons to be grateful, to appreciate, and to savor life even when it's challenging. It's a way of approaching life that allows you to find beauty, meaning, and peace in every moment, even the hard ones.

Redefining joy starts with understanding that it isn't about constant positivity. Life is full of ups and downs, and expecting to feel joyful all the time sets you up for disappointment. Joy isn't about ignoring difficulties; it's about choosing to find meaning within them. It's the quiet appreciation for small moments, the ability to smile in the face of adversity, and the choice to see challenges as opportunities for growth. When you redefine joy as something that exists alongside life's struggles, you're giving yourself permission to experience life fully, without the pressure to be constantly "happy."

A powerful way to cultivate joy is to practice gratitude daily. Gratitude shifts your focus from what's lacking to what's present, reminding you of the abundance in your life. Start by taking a few minutes each day to write down things you're grateful for, no matter how small. It could be the warmth of your morning coffee, a kind word from a friend, or simply the fact that you made it through another day. Gratitude opens your eyes to the blessings that surround you, helping you find joy in even the most ordinary moments. When you're grateful, you're more likely to experience joy because you're recognizing the beauty in what already is.

Mindfulness is also essential in choosing joy. Often, we're so caught up in worries about the future or regrets about the past that we miss the joy available to us in the present moment. Mindfulness is about slowing down, taking a breath, and being fully engaged with what's happening right now. Whether it's the taste of a meal, the sound of laughter, or the warmth of the sun, mindfulness helps you connect with life as it is, not as you wish it were. When you practice mindfulness, you're choosing to be present with yourself, finding joy in the simplicity and richness of each moment.

Another key to choosing joy is letting go of comparison. Comparison steals joy by making you feel inadequate or dissatisfied with your own life. It's easy to get caught up in what others are doing, to feel like you're not achieving enough, or to believe that joy lies in reaching certain milestones. But joy isn't found in having what others have; it's found in appreciating your own journey. Each time you catch yourself comparing, remind yourself that your life is unique, that your experiences are meaningful, and that joy is something you create for yourself.

Letting go of comparison frees you to live authentically, to find joy in your own way, on your own terms.

Choosing joy also means embracing impermanence. Life is constantly changing, and clinging to any one moment—whether good or bad—only creates frustration. Joy is about accepting the ebb and flow of life, allowing yourself to experience each moment fully, knowing that it, too, will pass. When you embrace impermanence, you're free to find joy without fear of loss or disappointment. You're able to appreciate each experience for what it is, knowing that both joy and sorrow are part of life's natural rhythm. Impermanence teaches you to live in the present, to cherish moments as they come, and to let go when it's time.

A practical exercise to cultivate joy is the "Joy Jar." Each day, write down something that brought you joy—an accomplishment, a moment of laughter, or a small success—and place it in the jar. Over time, you'll build a collection of joyful moments that serve as a reminder of the abundance in your life. On days when joy feels hard to find, return to your Joy Jar, and read through these moments. This practice not only reinforces the habit of noticing joy but also reminds you that even on difficult days, joy is still there, waiting to be recognized and appreciated.

Finally, choosing joy means prioritizing self-care. You can't experience joy if you're constantly running on empty. Self-care isn't selfish; it's necessary for your well-being and for your ability to find joy in life. Take time to rest, to nourish your body and mind, and to do things that make you feel whole. When you prioritize self-care, you're creating a foundation for joy, one that supports you in being present, resilient, and open to life's beauty. Self-care helps you recharge, making it easier to find joy even in the smallest moments.

Because here's the truth: joy isn't something that just happens; it's something you choose. It's a decision to see life with a grateful heart, to live fully in the present, and to find meaning in every experience. When you choose joy, you're creating a life that's vibrant, a life that feels whole and abundant, regardless of what's going on around you. And in that choice, you're choosing a life that's truly worth living.

Joy doesn't need to come from big events or grand achievements; in fact, some of the purest joy is found in the small, everyday moments. We often overlook these simple pleasures in pursuit of something bigger, assuming that fulfillment lies somewhere on the horizon, waiting to be discovered. But life isn't made up of endless milestones; it's made up of ordinary moments. Choosing to find joy in these small, everyday experiences is what leads to a truly fulfilling life, one where you're present, engaged, and appreciative of each moment for what it is.

One of the simplest ways to find joy in the everyday is to cultivate a sense of wonder. Approach the world with the curiosity of a child, noticing things that might usually go unseen. Take time to appreciate the colors of a sunset, the rhythm of rain on a window, or the taste of a meal made with care. When you allow yourself to experience life through a lens of wonder, you're finding beauty in places that others may overlook. Wonder brings joy because it connects you to the present moment, reminding you that each day holds something worth noticing, worth appreciating.

Another key to finding joy in everyday life is to create routines that you genuinely enjoy. Sometimes, joy comes from the familiarity of a routine that brings you comfort and peace. Whether it's a morning coffee ritual, an evening walk, or time spent journaling, these small, intentional routines create anchors throughout your day, moments to pause, reflect, and reconnect with yourself. Joyful routines bring structure, yes, but they also serve as reminders to slow down and savor life, to find satisfaction in the rhythm of your days. By creating routines that bring you joy, you're transforming ordinary moments into meaningful ones.

Practicing gratitude throughout the day also helps you find joy in the everyday. You don't have to wait until the end of the day to reflect on what you're grateful for. Pause throughout your day to acknowledge what's bringing you joy right now, whether it's a moment of quiet, a good conversation, or the feeling of the sun on your skin. Gratitude in real time allows you to experience joy as it's happening, helping you feel connected to the present rather than always rushing ahead. By practicing gratitude in the moment, you're building a habit of finding joy in every part of your day.

Connecting with others is also a powerful source of everyday joy. A life filled with small, meaningful interactions is one that feels rich, no matter how simple the connections might seem. Send a thoughtful message, share a laugh, or spend a few extra moments in a conversation with someone you care about. Human connection brings joy because it reminds you that you're not alone, that life is shared, and that each interaction is a chance to give and receive something meaningful. By investing in small, everyday connections, you're creating a life that feels joyful, grounded, and deeply connected.

Another way to find joy in the everyday is to be fully present in your activities, even the seemingly mundane ones. We often go through daily tasks on autopilot, rushing through them to get to something "more important." But even routine activities—washing dishes, folding laundry, or tidying up—can bring a sense of joy and peace when done mindfully. Focus on the sensations, the movements, the rhythm of each task. When you're fully present, even the most routine activities become an opportunity for joy, a way to engage with life instead of rushing past it.

Choosing to laugh, even at the small absurdities of life, is another way to bring joy into every day. Life is full of moments that can either frustrate or amuse, depending on your perspective. When things don't go as planned, when you make a silly mistake, or when the day feels overwhelming, find a way to laugh about it. Humor brings lightness, a reminder not to take everything too seriously. Each time you choose laughter over frustration, you're reinforcing joy as a habit, a way of looking at life that prioritizes resilience over stress.

Finally, finding joy in the everyday means letting go of the need for everything to be perfect. Joy isn't found in a flawless day or a perfectly executed plan; it's found in the messy, unexpected, and real moments of life. When you let go of perfectionism, you're giving yourself permission to enjoy things as they are, without constantly striving to improve or control. Embrace the imperfections, the moments that don't go as planned, and recognize that joy often comes from the unexpected. Life's beauty isn't in perfection; it's in the way it unfolds naturally, imperfectly, and often surprisingly.

Because here's the truth: a fulfilling life isn't made up of a few grand moments; it's built on countless small ones. When you find joy in the everyday, you're choosing a life that feels rich, vibrant, and meaningful no matter what's happening around you. By embracing these simple pleasures, you're creating a life that's full of presence, appreciation, and a quiet, lasting joy—a joy that doesn't depend on circumstances but grows from within.

Joy doesn't need to come from big events or grand achievements; in fact, some of the purest joy is found in the small, everyday moments. We often overlook these simple pleasures in pursuit of something bigger, assuming that fulfillment lies somewhere on the horizon, waiting to be discovered. But life isn't made up of endless milestones; it's made up of ordinary moments. Choosing to find joy in these small, everyday experiences is what leads to a truly fulfilling life, one where you're present, engaged, and appreciative of each moment for what it is.

One of the simplest ways to find joy in the everyday is to cultivate a sense of wonder. Approach the world with the curiosity of a child, noticing things that might usually go unseen. Take time to appreciate the colors of a sunset, the rhythm of rain on a window, or the taste of a meal made with care. When you allow yourself to experience life through a lens of wonder, you're finding beauty in places that others may overlook. Wonder brings joy because it connects you to the present moment, reminding you that each day holds something worth noticing, worth appreciating.

Another key to finding joy in everyday life is to create routines that you genuinely enjoy. Sometimes, joy comes from the familiarity of a routine that brings you comfort and peace. Whether it's a morning coffee ritual, an evening walk, or time spent journaling, these small, intentional routines create anchors throughout your day, moments to pause, reflect, and reconnect with yourself. Joyful routines bring structure, yes, but they also serve as reminders to slow down and savor life, to find satisfaction in the rhythm of your days. By creating routines that bring you joy, you're transforming ordinary moments into meaningful ones.

Practicing gratitude throughout the day also helps you find joy in the everyday. You don't have to wait until the end of the day to reflect on what you're grateful for. Pause throughout your day to acknowledge what's bringing you joy right now, whether it's a moment of quiet, a good conversation, or the feeling of the sun on your skin. Gratitude in real time allows you to experience joy as it's happening, helping you feel connected to the present rather than always rushing ahead. By practicing gratitude in the moment, you're building a habit of finding joy in every part of your day.

Connecting with others is also a powerful source of everyday joy. A life filled with small, meaningful interactions is one that feels rich, no matter how simple the connections might seem. Send a thoughtful message, share a laugh, or spend a few extra moments in a conversation with someone you care about. Human connection brings joy because it reminds you that you're not alone, that life is shared, and that each interaction is a chance to give and receive something meaningful. By investing in small, everyday connections, you're creating a life that feels joyful, grounded, and deeply connected.

Another way to find joy in the everyday is to be fully present in your activities, even the seemingly mundane ones. We often go through daily tasks on autopilot, rushing through them to get to something "more important." But even routine activities—washing dishes, folding laundry, or tidying up—can bring a sense of joy and peace when done mindfully. Focus on the sensations, the movements, the rhythm of each task. When you're fully present, even the most routine activities become an opportunity for joy, a way to engage with life instead of rushing past it.

Choosing to laugh, even at the small absurdities of life, is another way to bring joy into every day. Life is full of moments that can either frustrate or amuse, depending on your perspective. When things don't go as planned, when you make a silly mistake, or when the day feels overwhelming, find a way to laugh about it. Humor brings lightness, a reminder not to take everything too seriously. Each time you choose laughter over frustration, you're reinforcing joy as a habit, a way of looking at life that prioritizes resilience over stress.

Finally, finding joy in the everyday means letting go of the need for everything to be perfect. Joy isn't found in a flawless day or a perfectly executed plan; it's found in the messy, unexpected, and real moments of life. When you let go of perfectionism, you're giving yourself permission to enjoy things as they are, without constantly striving to improve or control. Embrace the imperfections, the moments that don't go as planned, and recognize that joy often comes from the unexpected. Life's beauty isn't in perfection; it's in the way it unfolds naturally, imperfectly, and often surprisingly.

Because here's the truth: a fulfilling life isn't made up of a few grand moments; it's built on countless small ones. When you find joy in the everyday, you're choosing a life that feels rich, vibrant, and meaningful no matter what's happening around you. By embracing these simple pleasures, you're creating a life that's full of presence, appreciation, and a quiet, lasting joy—a joy that doesn't depend on circumstances but grows from within.

Joy doesn't have to be a rare experience or something you stumble upon by chance. When you make joy a daily practice, it becomes a consistent part of your life—a way of approaching each day with openness, gratitude, and a sense of wonder. Practicing joy daily isn't about ignoring life's challenges; it's about choosing to find moments of light, even in the midst of them. It's about creating habits, routines, and mindsets that allow joy to thrive, making it a regular part of your experience rather than something you feel only occasionally.

One of the most powerful ways to practice joy daily is through gratitude. Start each day by listing a few things you're grateful for. They don't have to be big or profound; sometimes, the smallest things bring the greatest joy. Perhaps it's the way sunlight filters through your window, the taste of a favorite breakfast, or the comforting presence of someone you love. By beginning your day with gratitude, you're setting a positive tone, a reminder to appreciate what you have rather than focus on what's missing. This habit shifts your mindset to one that naturally seeks joy, finding reasons to be thankful no matter what the day brings.

Engaging in creative activities also brings daily joy. Creativity connects you to a playful, curious side of yourself that often goes overlooked in day-to-day life. Whether it's painting, writing, cooking, or dancing, find an activity that allows you to express yourself freely. Creative expression is a way to engage with life more deeply, to bring joy into your routine in a way that feels light and fun. Creativity reminds you that joy isn't something you have to find; it's something you can create, a spark of self-expression that adds color and meaning to your day.

Connecting with nature is another simple way to practice joy. Spending even a few minutes outside, whether it's taking a walk, tending to a plant, or simply observing the world around you, brings a sense of calm and wonder. Nature has a way of grounding you, of reminding you that joy is found in the simplest things—the rustle of leaves, the feel of grass underfoot, the sound of birdsong. When you make nature a regular part of your routine, you're giving yourself a break from screens, schedules, and stress, reconnecting with something larger and more peaceful. Nature invites you to slow down, to breathe, and to feel joy in the present moment.

Practicing acts of kindness is also a powerful source of joy. Joy isn't just something you experience; it's something you share. Each day, look for ways to brighten someone else's day—a kind word, a small favor, or even a simple smile. Kindness connects you to others, creating a cycle of joy that flows both ways. When you bring joy to others, you're also nurturing your own sense of happiness, knowing that you're contributing something positive to the world. Acts of kindness don't have to be grand gestures; even the smallest acts make a difference, creating a ripple effect that spreads joy in ways you may never see.

Mindfulness is essential in making joy a lasting part of your life. Often, we rush through our days, focused on what's next rather than what's now. Mindfulness encourages you to pause, to savor each moment, and to experience life more fully. Whether it's savoring a meal, listening intently to someone, or simply noticing your own breath, mindfulness helps you connect with the present. When you practice mindfulness, joy becomes less about finding "big" moments and more about appreciating what's right in front of you. It's about realizing that joy isn't in the future or the past—it's in this very moment, if you're willing to be fully present with it.

Incorporating moments of play is also essential for daily joy. As adults, we often lose touch with the playful side of ourselves, forgetting that joy is naturally found in fun and spontaneity. Give yourself permission to be playful each day, to let go of seriousness, and to do something just because it's enjoyable. Play isn't frivolous; it's a way of reconnecting with the joy that comes from being fully engaged, without pressure or purpose. Whether it's a game, a hobby, or a silly activity, play reminds you to take life a little less seriously, to enjoy the moment simply because it feels good.

Finally, make joy a part of your self-talk. Often, our inner dialogue is filled with criticism, doubt, or worry, which naturally blocks joy. Each day, practice speaking to yourself with kindness, encouragement, and appreciation. Tell yourself, *I am worthy of joy. I choose to find beauty in today. I am grateful for this life.* Positive self-talk creates a mindset where joy feels natural and deserved, where you're open to joy because you believe you're worthy of it. When you practice self-compassion, you're nurturing a mindset that allows joy to flourish, one where you see yourself not as a critic but as a source of support.

Because here's the truth: joy isn't just something that happens to you; it's something you cultivate. By practicing joy daily, you're choosing to build a life that feels fulfilling, a life that's rooted in gratitude, kindness, and presence. When joy becomes a regular part of your day, you're creating a life that's not only happier but richer, more vibrant, and full of meaning. And that's what joy is—a choice to engage deeply with life, to appreciate each moment, and to live with a heart open to all the beauty that surrounds you.

# Chapter 19:
# Embracing Peace

Peace isn't found in the absence of challenges; it's found in the way you respond to them. True peace is an inner state, a sense of calm and acceptance that you carry with you no matter what's going on around you. Embracing peace means choosing to create a sanctuary within yourself, a place you can return to for strength, comfort, and clarity when life feels chaotic. Cultivating inner peace allows you to approach life with a clear mind, a steady heart, and a resilience that doesn't depend on circumstances.

The journey to inner peace starts with acceptance. Life is full of ups and downs, unexpected changes, and challenges. Resisting what you can't control only creates tension, keeping you in a state of anxiety and frustration. Acceptance doesn't mean giving up; it means recognizing what's beyond your control and choosing to let go of the need to change it. By practicing acceptance, you're allowing yourself to be present with life as it is, not as you wish it were. This simple shift brings a sense of ease, a release of the constant struggle to "fix" or "fight" against what you can't change. Inner peace is found in this acceptance, in the choice to be fully present with whatever is unfolding.

Another powerful practice for cultivating inner peace is meditation. Meditation is a way of quieting the mind, a chance to connect with the present moment without judgment. Even a few minutes of meditation each day can create a sense of calm, helping you release tension and reconnect with yourself. Meditation teaches you to observe your thoughts without becoming attached to them, to let go of mental clutter, and to create a mental space that's free from the noise of worry and stress. As you build a meditation practice, you're building a foundation of peace that's always available, a quiet place you can return to whenever you need it.

Mindful breathing is also essential in embracing inner peace. Often, we hold our breath or breathe shallowly when we're stressed, which only increases feelings of anxiety. Taking deep, mindful breaths calms the nervous system, brings oxygen to the body, and creates an immediate sense of grounding. Try a simple breathing exercise: inhale deeply for a count of four, hold for four, and exhale for four. This practice reminds you that peace is always available through your breath, that with each deep breath, you're choosing calm over chaos, presence over panic.

Letting go of perfectionism is another crucial step toward inner peace. Perfectionism keeps you in a constant state of dissatisfaction, always striving, never feeling "enough." Peace doesn't come from flawless performance; it comes from embracing yourself as you are. When you release the need to be perfect, you're freeing yourself to experience life fully, without the constant pressure to measure up. Let go of the unrealistic expectations, the need for approval, and the relentless pursuit of "better." Instead, choose self-compassion, recognizing that peace is found in being enough exactly as you are.

Another way to cultivate peace within is through self-reflection. Taking time to check in with yourself, to process your emotions, and to understand your needs creates an internal balance. Self-reflection helps you identify what might be causing stress or unease, allowing you to address it rather than let it fester. Journaling, meditation, or simply taking a quiet moment to ask yourself, *How am I feeling today?* creates a space where you can process and release what's on your mind. By honoring your emotions and allowing yourself to feel them fully, you're creating a relationship with yourself that's rooted in understanding and peace.

Setting boundaries is also essential in maintaining inner peace. Peace isn't just something you create within yourself; it's something you protect. Boundaries allow you to safeguard your energy, to limit negative influences, and to create a space where you feel safe and respected. Whether it's setting boundaries with work, social commitments, or relationships, boundaries allow you to prioritize your peace without guilt. When you honor your limits, you're reinforcing the belief that your well-being matters, that you're worthy of peace, and that protecting it is a priority.

Finally, embrace the power of gratitude to foster inner peace. Gratitude shifts your focus from what's lacking to what's present, reminding you of the abundance in your life. Each time you practice gratitude, you're choosing to see the positives, to appreciate what's here rather than worry about what's missing. Gratitude creates a mental state of peace, a recognition that you have enough, that you are enough, and that there is beauty in each day. By practicing gratitude, you're reinforcing a mindset that allows peace to flourish, even in the face of challenges.

Because here's the truth: peace isn't found in perfect circumstances; it's found in a calm, accepting heart. When you cultivate peace within, you're building a life that's resilient, a life that feels steady even when the world around you feels chaotic. Inner peace is a choice, a commitment to nurturing calm, clarity, and compassion within yourself. And when you embrace this peace, you're creating a foundation for a life that's not only joyful but profoundly grounded, a life that flows with ease rather than struggle.

Peace doesn't only exist within us; it's something we choose to cultivate in our relationships. While life inevitably brings misunderstandings and disagreements, the way we respond determines whether we create drama or preserve harmony. Choosing peace over drama isn't about avoiding conflict entirely—it's about handling conflict in a way that strengthens rather than fractures connections. When you choose to prioritize harmony, you're building relationships rooted in respect, understanding, and empathy. Choosing peace over drama is a way of creating an environment where both you and others feel safe, valued, and seen.

One of the most powerful steps to maintaining harmony in relationships is practicing active listening. Often, conflict arises because we're not really hearing the other person; we're focused on defending ourselves, proving our point, or winning the argument. Active listening means setting aside your own agenda, being present, and truly understanding the other person's perspective. Instead of interrupting or planning your response, take a moment to listen without judgment. This simple act of listening not only diffuses tension but also shows respect, a willingness to understand rather than to dominate. When people feel heard, they're more likely to respond with openness and calm, creating a space where peace can thrive.

Another way to choose peace is to learn how to pause before reacting. In heated moments, it's easy to say things you don't mean or to escalate a situation unintentionally. By taking a pause—a deep breath, a short moment to gather your thoughts—you're giving yourself time to respond rather than react. This pause allows you to choose words and actions that align with your values rather than with the emotion of the moment. It's a reminder that peace is a choice, one you make by staying calm and choosing responses that build rather than tear down. Each pause is a step toward harmony, a decision to let peace guide your actions.

Setting boundaries around conversations is also essential for choosing peace. Not every topic needs to be discussed, and not every person will understand your perspective. Boundaries allow you to protect your peace by choosing which conversations are worth engaging in and which are best left alone. If a topic feels too charged, too triggering, or unproductive, gently steer the conversation in a different direction or express your need to step away. Boundaries aren't about avoiding others; they're about protecting your energy, choosing peace over prolonged conflict, and maintaining a sense of control over the conversations you engage in.

Letting go of the need to be "right" is another key to choosing peace in relationships. Often, drama arises because we're invested in proving our point, in making others see things our way. But prioritizing harmony over being right means recognizing that some disagreements don't need to be resolved; sometimes, the most peaceful path is to agree to disagree. Let go of the need to "win" an argument, and instead focus on maintaining mutual respect. When you release the attachment to being right, you're creating space for acceptance, for the possibility of understanding without full agreement. In that space, peace becomes more important than the argument itself.

Practicing empathy is also essential for choosing peace over drama. Empathy allows you to see things from the other person's perspective, to understand why they might be feeling hurt, angry, or misunderstood. When you approach conflict with empathy, you're less likely to react defensively and more likely to respond with kindness. Instead of assuming the worst, ask yourself what might be driving their feelings, what they might need from the conversation, or what fears or insecurities they're experiencing. Empathy softens your response, helping you approach even the most challenging interactions with compassion. This choice creates an environment where peace, not conflict, can flourish.

Another effective way to reduce drama is to choose your battles wisely. Not every disagreement is worth engaging in, and sometimes the most peaceful choice is to simply let something go. Ask yourself, *Is this worth my energy? Will this matter in a week, a month, or a year?* Choosing to let go of minor irritations, misunderstandings, or criticisms is an act of grace, a decision to keep the bigger picture in mind. When you choose your battles carefully, you're protecting your peace, ensuring that your energy goes toward what truly matters rather than being drained by minor conflicts.

Lastly, practicing forgiveness helps you create lasting harmony in relationships. Holding onto grudges, past mistakes, or unresolved issues only fuels drama, keeping you stuck in cycles of resentment. Forgiveness doesn't mean forgetting or condoning what happened; it means choosing to release the weight of past conflicts. By forgiving, you're choosing peace over bitterness, allowing both yourself and the other person to move forward. Forgiveness isn't just an act of kindness toward others; it's a gift of freedom you give yourself. When you practice forgiveness, you're creating relationships that are resilient, built on a foundation of peace rather than tension.

Because here's the truth: choosing peace in relationships is a choice to prioritize harmony, understanding, and respect over temporary emotions. When you approach others with a commitment to peace, you're creating connections that feel safe, fulfilling, and truly meaningful. Drama fades, but peace endures, creating relationships that aren't only calm but deeply rooted in kindness, empathy, and mutual respect. And that's where real, lasting harmony is found—in the choice to live with peace as your guiding value.

Peace isn't just a feeling; it's something you can cultivate in your surroundings. The spaces where you live, work, and spend time deeply impact your sense of calm, affecting your mental clarity, mood, and energy. Creating a peaceful environment isn't about having an expensive home or perfect decor; it's about making intentional choices that reflect a calm, supportive atmosphere. When you design your environment with peace in mind, you're creating a sanctuary that helps you recharge, reconnect, and feel at ease. It's a way to bring a sense of calm into every day, a reminder that peace is something you can create right where you are.

One of the most effective ways to create a peaceful environment is to declutter. Physical clutter often leads to mental clutter, filling your space with unnecessary distractions that keep you from fully relaxing. Take time to go through your belongings, keeping only what truly adds value or meaning to your life. The goal isn't to live with as little as possible, but to remove anything that no longer serves a purpose. By clearing out the excess, you're making space for calm, creating a visual environment that feels clean, open, and refreshing. Decluttering isn't just about your belongings; it's about letting go of what you don't need, a physical act that reflects an inner choice for simplicity and clarity.

Incorporating natural elements into your space is also essential for creating peace. Nature has a calming effect, grounding you and reminding you of the beauty outside your daily routines. Consider adding plants, flowers, or natural materials like wood, stone, or water features. Plants not only purify the air but bring a sense of life and growth into your environment, adding visual softness and tranquility. Even small touches—a vase of fresh flowers, a collection of stones, or a bowl of shells—bring the calming energy of nature indoors. These elements create a space that feels balanced, connecting you to the peaceful rhythms of the natural world.

Lighting is another powerful factor in cultivating a peaceful environment. Bright, harsh lighting can feel overwhelming, while soft, warm lighting creates a sense of calm and relaxation. Make use of natural light whenever possible, letting in sunlight to energize and brighten your space. In the evenings, opt for dimmable lights, candles, or soft lamp lighting to create a cozy, peaceful atmosphere. Experiment with lighting to find what feels most calming to you, transforming your space from simply functional to restorative. Lighting that adapts to your needs helps you transition from busy moments to restful ones, enhancing the sense of peace in your surroundings.

Using calming colors can also transform the energy of your space. Colors have a psychological impact, influencing your mood and mental state. Soft, neutral tones—like shades of blue, green, gray, or beige—tend to create a calming atmosphere, evoking a sense of openness and ease. While everyone has their own color preferences, choosing tones that bring a feeling of comfort and relaxation can help you create a space that feels welcoming and peaceful. If a full room makeover isn't possible, consider adding calming colors in small ways: throw pillows, rugs, blankets, or artwork. These subtle shifts add warmth and peace to your space, allowing you to feel more at home.

Another key to creating a peaceful environment is incorporating personal touches that reflect your values and bring you joy. These items don't have to be expensive or impressive; they simply need to resonate with you. It could be a meaningful piece of art, a favorite book, family photos, or mementos from memorable experiences. These personal items create a sense of connection and familiarity, grounding you in what's most important to you. When your environment reflects your personality and values, it becomes a space that feels like yours—a sanctuary that welcomes and restores you.

Creating designated "quiet zones" can also enhance the peacefulness of your environment. A quiet zone doesn't need to be a whole room; it can be a small corner with a cozy chair, a reading nook, or even a small meditation space with a mat or cushion. This area serves as a retreat, a place where you can step away from distractions and find peace. Use this space for reading, meditating, or simply unwinding. By having a dedicated area for relaxation, you're making peace a priority, a part of your daily life that's always available, even on busy days.

Finally, use soothing sounds and scents to cultivate a peaceful atmosphere. Sound has a powerful impact on mood, so consider playing calming music, nature sounds, or ambient noise that promotes relaxation. Similarly, scents like lavender, chamomile, eucalyptus, or vanilla can create a calming effect, helping you feel more at ease. Whether you use candles, essential oils, or incense, these small additions transform your space into a sensory experience, one that invites you to relax and recharge. Sounds and scents create an immersive environment, helping you to fully unwind and embrace a sense of peace.

Because here's the truth: your environment shapes your experience. When you create a space that feels calm, supportive, and reflective of who you are, you're building a sanctuary that supports your well-being. A peaceful environment isn't just about aesthetics; it's about nurturing a space that helps you feel balanced, grounded, and at home. By cultivating peace in your surroundings, you're creating a foundation for a life that feels restful, joyful, and truly yours.

The world can feel chaotic, overwhelming, and full of demands on your attention. News cycles, social media, and daily stressors can easily pull you away from your sense of inner calm, filling your mind with worry, distraction, and a sense of urgency. Protecting your peace means setting boundaries with the outside world, intentionally choosing what you let in and how you respond. When you make peace a priority, you're creating a buffer between yourself and the chaos, allowing you to maintain a sense of calm and focus no matter what's happening around you.

One of the most effective ways to protect your peace is to limit your exposure to news and social media. While staying informed is important, constant exposure to negative news and curated images of others' lives can drain your energy and erode your sense of peace. Set limits on your media consumption, choosing specific times to check in rather than allowing constant notifications. Be mindful of what you're absorbing, filtering out content that triggers stress or anxiety. When you're selective about what you let in, you're protecting your mental and emotional space, making room for calm rather than chaos.

Setting boundaries with people is also essential for protecting your peace. Not everyone respects personal boundaries, and some relationships can be draining or disruptive to your well-being. Protecting your peace means knowing when to say "no," when to walk away, and when to prioritize your needs over others' demands. Boundaries aren't about shutting people out; they're about choosing relationships that support, respect, and uplift you. When you set boundaries, you're sending a message that your peace matters, that you're willing to prioritize your well-being even if it means difficult conversations or decisions.

Another powerful tool for maintaining peace is practicing emotional detachment. Emotional detachment doesn't mean becoming indifferent or uncaring; it means learning not to be overly affected by external situations. When you detach, you're able to witness what's happening without feeling personally threatened or overwhelmed. This detachment creates a mental buffer, allowing you to observe without absorbing every emotion around you. By practicing emotional detachment, you're choosing to maintain your inner calm, recognizing that you can care without letting outside chaos disrupt your peace.

Building a mindfulness practice also helps you protect your peace. When you're mindful, you're more aware of your thoughts, emotions, and reactions, giving you the ability to pause rather than react impulsively. This pause allows you to respond with intention, choosing actions that support your peace. Whether it's taking deep breaths, a short meditation, or simply checking in with yourself, mindfulness brings you back to the present, grounding you in calm rather than being swept up by external stressors. Mindfulness allows you to approach each situation with clarity, reducing the impact of outside chaos on your inner state.

Engaging in regular self-care is essential for protecting your peace. Self-care isn't just about relaxation; it's about replenishing your energy, honoring your needs, and creating resilience against stress. When you take time to care for your physical, emotional, and mental well-being, you're strengthening your foundation of peace. Self-care practices like exercise, sleep, healthy eating, and time in nature help you stay balanced, making it easier to navigate life's demands without losing your calm. Self-care is an act of self-respect, a way of saying that your peace is worth investing in.

Practicing discernment with your time and energy is another way to protect your peace. Not every opportunity, event, or relationship requires your attention. By being selective with where you spend your time and energy, you're ensuring that you're focused on what truly matters. Discernment means evaluating what adds value to your life and letting go of what drains you. It's about making choices that align with your values and purpose, reducing the noise of unnecessary distractions. When you practice discernment, you're prioritizing quality over quantity, choosing activities and people that contribute to your peace.

Lastly, embrace the power of letting go to protect your peace. Often, we hold onto past mistakes, regrets, or unresolved situations, carrying the weight of things we can't change. Letting go means releasing the need for control, accepting that not everything is within your power. Whether it's forgiving yourself, releasing resentment, or letting go of unmet expectations, this act creates space for peace. When you let go, you're choosing to free yourself from the burden of the past, allowing yourself to live more fully in the present. Letting go isn't just about moving on; it's about creating a mental and emotional space where peace can flourish.

Because here's the truth: protecting your peace is an active choice, a commitment to live intentionally rather than reactively. When you protect your peace, you're creating a life that feels grounded, one where you're not constantly pulled by external demands. You're choosing to build a foundation of calm, a sense of strength that allows you to face life with clarity, resilience, and joy. And in that choice, you're creating a life that's not just peaceful, but deeply, authentically yours.

# Chapter 20:
# Creating a Legacy

Legacy isn't just what you leave behind; it's what you build every day through your actions, choices, and relationships. Creating a legacy means living with intention, aligning your life with values that reflect who you truly are and what you want to contribute to the world. It's about crafting a life that matters, a life that impacts others in ways that go beyond the surface. When you live with a legacy in mind, you're choosing to build something meaningful, a lasting impact that continues to resonate long after you're gone.

The first step in defining your legacy is identifying what you want to stand for. Legacy is rooted in your values, the principles you hold closest. Ask yourself, *What do I want to be remembered for?* Whether it's kindness, resilience, creativity, or service, your legacy reflects the essence of who you are. Take time to reflect on these core values, recognizing that they're the foundation upon which your legacy will be built. When you live in alignment with these values, you're creating a life that's not only fulfilling but deeply meaningful, a life that naturally leaves a positive impact.

Creating a legacy doesn't require fame, wealth, or ground-breaking achievements; it's about everyday actions. Each moment, each interaction, is an opportunity to live in a way that reflects your values. Sometimes, the most impactful legacies are built through small acts of kindness, patience, and compassion. A legacy is often created in how you treat others, how you handle adversity, and how you give back to the world around you. By focusing on the small, daily choices that align with your values, you're creating a legacy that feels authentic and accessible, one that anyone can aspire to, regardless of circumstances.

Another way to define your legacy is to think about the people you want to impact. Legacy is often relational, something that lives on in the people whose lives you've touched. Whether it's family, friends, coworkers, or a broader community, the relationships you build are an essential part of your legacy. How do you want to be remembered by these people? What lessons, support, or inspiration do you hope to offer them? By considering the impact you want to have on others, you're clarifying the kind of legacy you wish to create. Each connection, each word of encouragement, and each act of support builds a legacy that lives on in the lives of those you care about.

Your passions are also a significant part of your legacy. The things you're passionate about—whether it's art, social causes, education, or environmental protection—reflect your unique gifts and the ways you contribute to the world. When you pursue your passions with purpose, you're creating a legacy that inspires others to do the same. Think about how your interests, talents, or causes can leave a positive impact, how they can serve as a source of inspiration for others to follow their own paths. Your legacy doesn't have to look like anyone else's; it's about embracing what makes you unique and sharing that passion in a way that feels genuine.

Legacy is also about resilience, about how you overcome challenges and what you teach others through your journey. Often, people are remembered not just for what they accomplished but for how they faced adversity. Your legacy includes the ways you handle setbacks, the resilience you show in difficult times, and the hope you give to others by refusing to give up. When you embrace resilience, you're showing others that it's possible to grow through hardship, to find meaning in struggles, and to emerge stronger. This strength becomes a part of your legacy, a testament to the power of perseverance and inner strength.

Lastly, defining your legacy means choosing to live with gratitude. A life of gratitude is one that naturally impacts others, creating an atmosphere of appreciation and generosity. When you express gratitude, you're reinforcing the importance of kindness, the beauty of each moment, and the value of each person you encounter. Gratitude is a gift that continues to give, a way of living that inspires others to cherish their own lives. By living with gratitude, you're creating a legacy of positivity, one that spreads joy, warmth, and a deep appreciation for the simple things that make life beautiful.

Because here's the truth: legacy isn't something you wait to create; it's something you build every day. When you live with intention, aligning your actions with your values, you're creating a legacy that feels genuine, impactful, and fulfilling. Legacy isn't just about what you achieve; it's about who you are, what you stand for, and how you make others feel. And when you define your legacy with clarity and purpose, you're creating a life that matters, a life that resonates, and a life that leaves a positive mark on the world.

Legacy isn't built in a single moment; it's woven into the small, intentional choices you make every day. Living with purpose means approaching each day with a sense of intention, choosing actions that reflect your values, and pursuing goals that feel meaningful. When you live with purpose, you're not just drifting through life; you're creating a legacy, piece by piece, with every decision. Purpose gives direction to your life, turning ordinary days into something powerful, something that matters not only to you but to those around you.

One of the simplest ways to live with purpose is to start each day with a clear intention. This doesn't have to be something grand or complicated; sometimes, it's as simple as choosing to be kind, to listen deeply, or to express gratitude. Setting an intention each morning grounds you, reminding you of what truly matters. It brings clarity and focus to your day, helping you to align your actions with your values. When you approach each day with a purposeful intention, you're building a life that reflects who you truly are, creating a legacy of authenticity, integrity, and kindness.

Another way to live with purpose is to approach your work, no matter what it is, with passion and dedication. Legacy isn't limited to certain careers or roles; it's about how you show up in whatever you do. Whether it's your career, your hobbies, or your family life, purpose is found in doing things wholeheartedly. Approach each task, each interaction, with a sense of pride, knowing that your efforts contribute to something meaningful. When you pour energy and care into your work, you're building a legacy that shows others the value of commitment, the joy of doing something well, and the impact of giving your best.

Practicing kindness daily is also essential in creating a legacy of purpose. Kindness may seem like a small thing, but it has a ripple effect, touching lives in ways you may never see. Choose to be compassionate, to offer a smile, or to lend a hand when you can. These small acts of kindness build a legacy of love and respect, showing others that every interaction matters. When you lead with kindness, you're creating an environment of peace, understanding, and support. People remember how you made them feel, and by making kindness a habit, you're leaving a legacy that others will carry forward.

Living with purpose also means staying aligned with your goals. Purpose isn't only about grand ambitions; it's about the goals that bring you a sense of fulfillment. Take time to reflect on your goals, making sure they align with what you want to contribute to the world. Whether it's a personal project, a career aspiration, or a commitment to self-growth, purpose is strengthened when you pursue goals that resonate with your true self. Each goal, each step toward growth, adds to your legacy, creating a life that feels fulfilling, one where you're actively contributing to something meaningful.

Another important part of living with purpose is learning to say no. Legacy is built not only by what you do but by what you choose not to do. By setting boundaries around your time and energy, you're protecting your purpose, ensuring that your efforts are directed toward what truly matters. Saying no to distractions, unhealthy relationships, or activities that don't align with your values allows you to focus on what's most meaningful. When you protect your purpose, you're creating a legacy that's not scattered but intentional, one that's built on a clear sense of direction.

Reflecting on your day each evening is a powerful practice for living with purpose. Take a few moments to consider what went well, what you're proud of, and how you contributed to your legacy. This reflection helps you stay connected to your purpose, allowing you to celebrate your progress and learn from your challenges. When you reflect on your actions, you're reinforcing a mindset of growth, ensuring that each day contributes to a life of meaning. This nightly reflection is a small but powerful way to keep your legacy alive, a reminder that each day is an opportunity to live with intention.

Because here's the truth: legacy isn't a destination; it's the journey of living purposefully, day by day. When you infuse your daily actions with meaning, you're creating a life that doesn't just look good from the outside but feels fulfilling from within. Purpose gives life depth, turning each moment into something significant, each day into a part of your legacy. And when you live with purpose, you're creating a legacy that endures—a legacy that's built on love, integrity, and a commitment to leaving the world better than you found it.

A legacy is more than what you leave behind; it's the impact that continues to inspire others, the example that encourages future generations to live with purpose, courage, and compassion. When you inspire others, you're not just creating a memory—you're sparking a lasting ripple effect, a chain reaction of positive influence that lives on. Inspiring others doesn't require perfection or fame; it simply requires you to live in a way that reflects your values, shares your passions, and encourages those around you to do the same.

One of the most powerful ways to inspire others is by leading through example. Actions speak louder than words, and the way you live each day demonstrates what's possible to those around you. Whether it's showing resilience in the face of adversity, pursuing your passions wholeheartedly, or living with kindness and integrity, your choices set a silent example for others to follow. When you lead by example, you're teaching others that it's possible to live a life aligned with one's values, to overcome challenges, and to approach each day with purpose. This example becomes a blueprint, a guide that others can draw upon in their own journeys.

Sharing your story openly and authentically is also a powerful way to leave an inspiring legacy. Every experience you've had—every triumph, every setback—has shaped who you are, and sharing these moments can motivate others to overcome their own struggles. When you're open about your challenges, your fears, and your growth, you're showing others that they're not alone, that everyone has battles to face, and that resilience is possible. Authenticity resonates because it's real; it reminds others that life doesn't have to be perfect to be meaningful. By sharing your journey, you're creating a legacy that offers hope, courage, and connection.

Another way to inspire others is by mentoring, teaching, or simply supporting those who look up to you. Legacy is often found in relationships, in the quiet moments where you offer guidance, encouragement, or wisdom. Whether it's younger family members, friends, coworkers, or people in your community, mentorship allows you to pass on what you've learned, to share insights that can help others grow. Being a mentor doesn't mean having all the answers; it means being present, being willing to listen, and offering whatever you can to help others on their paths. This act of mentorship creates a legacy that lives on in the people you've helped, in the lessons they carry forward.

Living a life that aligns with your purpose and passions also inspires others. When people see you fully engaged in what you love, pursuing your goals with enthusiasm and dedication, they're encouraged to do the same. Passion is contagious; it motivates others to pursue their own dreams, to take risks, and to live without regrets. By showing that it's possible to follow your heart, you're leaving a legacy that inspires others to embrace their own paths. A legacy built on passion isn't about convincing others to follow in your exact footsteps; it's about encouraging them to find their own.

Expressing gratitude and appreciation daily creates a legacy that uplifts others. When you live with gratitude, you're constantly reminding those around you of life's beauty, even in the simplest moments. Gratitude is a form of positivity that inspires others to focus on what they have, rather than what they lack. When you express gratitude toward others—recognizing their kindness, their contributions, or simply their presence—you're lifting them up, showing them that they're valued. A life of gratitude is one that resonates long after you're gone, a legacy that reminds others to cherish each moment, each connection, and each act of kindness.

Empowering others to believe in themselves is perhaps one of the most enduring forms of legacy. Encouragement, support, and belief in someone else's potential can change the course of their life. When you make it a habit to lift others up, to remind them of their strengths and their worth, you're leaving a legacy that's rooted in empowerment. This doesn't require grand gestures; often, a few kind words, a little encouragement, or simply listening is enough. By choosing to empower those around you, you're creating a legacy that's not about you—it's about helping others become the best versions of themselves.

Because here's the truth: inspiring others is about showing up as your authentic self, living with purpose, and sharing what you've learned along the way. A legacy that inspires doesn't come from trying to be remembered; it comes from living a life that's so genuine, so full of purpose and passion, that it naturally leaves an impact. When you live in a way that encourages others, you're creating a legacy that endures—a legacy that continues to make a difference, that lives on in the lives you've touched, and that leaves the world a little brighter, a little kinder, and a little more hopeful.

---

Legacy isn't just about the life you live; it's about what you leave behind, something that continues to resonate long after you're gone. Creating a lasting legacy means finding ways to leave something meaningful, something that reflects your values and impact in a way that endures. Whether it's through your contributions, your relationships, or the lives you've touched, leaving a meaningful legacy is a way of ensuring that your presence, your values, and your impact carry forward. When you create a lasting legacy, you're giving a part of yourself to future generations, a gift that reminds them of what's possible, what's valuable, and what it means to live fully.

One of the most enduring ways to leave a legacy is through your work—whether it's creative, intellectual, or philanthropic. Writing a book, creating art, building a business, or supporting a cause are all ways of contributing something lasting to the world. These creations become a part of your legacy, something tangible that others can draw inspiration from. Consider what you're passionate about, what you can create that reflects your values, or how you can contribute to a cause that will outlive you. Your work doesn't have to be grand; it simply has to be meaningful. Even small contributions, when made with purpose, leave a lasting mark.

Another way to leave a legacy is by documenting your journey—sharing your thoughts, experiences, and insights with future generations. This could be through journaling, letters, or even recorded messages. These personal accounts give those who come after you a window into your life, a chance to learn from your experiences and to see the world from your perspective. Documenting your journey is a gift to your future family, friends, or anyone who might find value in your story. It's a way of saying, *This is what I've learned, and I want to share it with you.* Your story becomes a legacy, a way of connecting across time, reminding others of your wisdom, resilience, and humanity.

Philanthropy is another powerful way to leave a meaningful legacy. Giving back to your community, supporting causes you believe in, or establishing a foundation can have a lasting impact, one that reflects your values and commitment to making the world a better place. Philanthropy doesn't have to be about wealth; it's about contributing in ways that matter, whether it's through time, resources, or support. When you give back, you're leaving a legacy of kindness, generosity, and compassion, showing others that success isn't just about personal achievement but about uplifting others. Each act of giving, no matter how small, creates a ripple effect, inspiring others to continue your legacy of service.

Mentorship and teaching are also ways to create a legacy that lives on. When you invest in others, sharing your skills, knowledge, or guidance, you're passing down tools that they can use long after you're gone. Mentorship doesn't require formal training; it's simply about being willing to support, to listen, and to help others grow. Each person you mentor, each lesson you teach, becomes a part of your legacy, creating a positive influence that continues through their own actions. Mentorship is a way of creating something meaningful, a way of ensuring that what you've learned and experienced can benefit others, making your impact a continuous, living legacy.

Creating traditions within your family or community is another way to build a lasting legacy. Traditions bring people together, offering comfort, continuity, and a sense of belonging. Whether it's an annual gathering, a shared hobby, or a family ritual, traditions keep your memory alive in a meaningful way. These rituals become something others look forward to, a way of celebrating and remembering your presence. When you establish traditions that reflect your values, your interests, or your love for those around you, you're building a legacy that strengthens bonds, creating memories that live on through shared moments.

Lastly, leaving a legacy of kindness is one of the simplest yet most powerful ways to create something lasting. Acts of kindness, generosity, and compassion have a ripple effect, spreading positivity in ways you may never see. When you treat people with respect, uplift those around you, and lead with kindness, you're creating a legacy that's carried forward by each person you've touched. A legacy of kindness is one that endures, a way of impacting lives in subtle but profound ways. Even small acts of kindness add up, creating a legacy of love, empathy, and connection that resonates long after you're gone.

Because here's the truth: a meaningful legacy isn't about leaving behind fame or fortune; it's about leaving behind something that touches lives, something that adds to the world in a way that reflects who you are. Legacy is built through everyday choices, small acts of love, and contributions that may seem ordinary but leave an extraordinary impact. When you create a legacy of meaning, you're giving future generations a piece of yourself, a reminder that their lives matter, that they, too, can live with purpose, and that they are part of something bigger.

# Conclusion: The Legacy of Living Unbreakable

Writing this book, following the journey from the first book to this final page, has been nothing short of profound. It feels like leaving behind a piece of my soul, a reflection of every broken moment that somehow paved the way to healing, every triumph born out of struggle, and every ounce of resilience that kept me grounded when life tried to tear me apart. If "I Won't Break" was the raw declaration of survival, of holding on through unimaginable pain, then this book, this follow-up, is the blueprint for transformation—for living, for choosing joy, peace, and meaning in every breath, for creating a life and legacy of purpose.

These two books together hold everything I know, every lesson life has taught me, every scar, every victory, and everything I've come to understand about how to survive and, ultimately, thrive. They're a record of my battles with abandonment, loss, love, and my fight for identity and freedom. I poured every ounce of truth into these pages not because I wanted the world to know my pain, but because I believe in the power of shared experience. I believe that by laying it all bare—by turning pain into something tangible, something honest and unfiltered—I could offer something meaningful to anyone who has ever felt like they, too, were breaking.

If this is the legacy I leave, if this is the culmination of my life's work, then I can close this chapter knowing I've given everything I had. And maybe, just maybe, these words will become more than stories. Maybe they'll be reminders to others that they're not alone, that survival is possible, and that healing—though messy, raw, and often unpredictable—can transform us in ways we never thought possible.

Book one was, above all else, a reckoning. It was an unmasking, a way of facing the darkest truths of my past, of breaking open the story of who I am and all I've endured. It was the survival manual, the "how" of enduring when everything in you wants to give up. In that book, I learned to confront the ghosts, to look pain in the eye, and to reclaim my own strength. But this second book—this book is where survival grows roots. This book is about the "what next"—about choosing to thrive, to rebuild, and to live a life of depth, presence, and intention.

Together, these two books create a bridge from darkness to light. Book one was survival; book two is transformation. They're the yin and yang, two halves of a journey that's still unfolding, because the truth is, healing is never linear. Growth is never finished. These books capture that essence—of survival evolving into resilience, of resilience blossoming into a life that isn't just lived but is loved. These books are my journey to peace, to purpose, and to finding a life I can call my own. And if they help even one person feel less alone, less defeated, then every moment was worth it.

Through these pages, I hope to have shown that life is a balancing act of struggle and beauty, of heartbreak and joy. I didn't write these books to promise anyone a perfect life or to pretend that pain disappears with a few positive thoughts. I wrote them to say that you can build a meaningful life even when it's messy. That you can be whole, even if some pieces are missing. That healing and thriving come not from erasing the past but from integrating it, from learning to live with it, to honor it as a part of who you are.

What you hold in your hands is a map. A map of what it means to survive, to heal, and to ultimately choose a life that feels rich, vibrant, and full of purpose. It's not a map that follows a single path—healing, growth, and peace are deeply personal journeys, ones that take unexpected turns and sometimes require us to walk alone. But it's a map that shows it's possible. That each step, however small, brings you closer to a life that is authentically yours, a life that holds meaning, joy, and fulfillment even in the face of challenges.

If this is my legacy, if these are the final words I leave behind, then let it be this: live unbreakable. Not because life won't try to break you—it will, in ways you may never see coming. But live unbreakable because resilience is a choice. Peace is a choice. Joy is a choice. And every single day, you have the power to choose who you are and what you stand for.

These books are my gift to you, the pieces of me that I hope will find a way into the hands and hearts of those who need it. They're my promise that no matter where you come from, no matter how lost you feel, there is a path forward. A path that can lead you to a life that is yours, a life that feels whole, a life that is lived fully, unapologetically, and without regret.

Maybe I'll write again. Maybe there will be more words to share, more insights to give as life unfolds in ways I haven't yet imagined. But if these are my last words, if these books stand as the culmination of everything I am, then I am at peace knowing they hold my truth, my journey, my unbreakable spirit. They hold everything I wish I'd known when I felt lost, broken, and alone. And they hold, above all, a message of hope: that healing is possible, that resilience is within you, and that every moment of survival can lead to a life of beauty, depth, and meaning.

Thank you for joining me on this journey. Thank you for reading, for allowing my words into your life, and for being a part of this legacy. May these words remind you that you are stronger than you know, that your story matters, and that every day is a chance to choose a life that is truly, wholly yours.

**Live unbreakable. This is my legacy—and now, it's yours too.**

## Author Biography

**Derrick Solano** doesn't write for the faint of heart. His work, his music, his words—they're all reflections of a life that's been dragged through hell, clawed its way out, and lived to tell the tale. Abandoned at two years old, bounced from foster homes to an adoptive family that stripped him of his identity, Derrick was given every reason to fade into the background, to let life break him. But he refused. Instead, he's made his pain into an anthem, his survival into a mission. With a past shaped by relentless trauma, addiction, and the kind of betrayal that would shatter most people, Derrick's writing doesn't sugarcoat. It's raw, it's unfiltered, and it speaks to the broken and the lost because he's been there—and he never hides that.

In his first book, *I Won't Break*, Derrick took readers on a harrowing journey of survival, showing them that resilience is forged in the fires of life's hardest blows. Now, with *Vexture*, he's doing more than telling his story; he's inviting you to find strength in yours. This book isn't just pages filled with words; it's a call to arms for anyone who's been cast aside, beaten down, or told they'll never be enough. Derrick writes from his own scars, his own battles, and he's unafraid to share the brutal truths that most people shy away from. His life isn't just an inspiration—it's a testament that no matter how deep the scars, there's always a way to rise.

When he's not putting his pain into words or lyrics, Derrick spends his time with his husband and their dogs, in a home built on love, honesty, and the relentless pursuit of truth. His story isn't over—it's just beginning, and he's bringing anyone who's willing to join him along for the ride.